About the Author

Brian Mayne is an inspirational speaker, au
presenting on an international stage. His core
improvement through the practice of personal Response-Ability
and purpose-led motivation have proven as effective and popular
with the corporate world as with the many individuals who come
to experienc is public presentations.

Having tr elled a path from gypsy origins and not being able
to read or wi properly, he became the owner of a nightclub
business that hed owing nearly £1,000,000, Brian developed
and used his simple techniques to transform himself, and re-
build his life. , as chairman of LIFT International, Brian has
been working i e field of personal development and corporate
training for the st eleven years and is becoming one of the
leading lights in e world of self-improvement.

For my father, a man who epitomized
the essence of Positive Thinking, Vision, and Goals.
In the words of Clarence Budinton Kelland:
'My father did not tell me how to live.
He lived, and let me watch him do it.'

BRIAN MAYNE'S

Goal
mapping

THE PRACTICAL WORKBOOK

How to Turn Your Dreams into Realities

WATKINS PUBLISHING

LONDON

This edition published in the UK 2006 by
Watkins Publishing, Sixth Floor, Castle House, 75-76 Wells Street,
London W1T 3QH

1 3 5 7 9 10 8 6 4 2

Designed and typeset by Jerry Goldie

Printed and bound in Great Britain

British Library Cataloguing in Publication data available

ISBN 1 84293 138 5

www.watkinspublishing.com

www.liftinternational.com

Contents

Are you in earnest, seek this very minute.

Whatever you can do, or dream you can, begin it.

Boldness has genius, power and magic in it.

Just begin and the mind grows heated.

Continue and the task will be completed.

FAUST

Acknowledgements

I would like to thank all those who have helped me on my path over the years, both the teachers and the students, whose names are too numerous to mention, but in particular a special thank you to my mother for her loving support through some of the darkest days of my life.

Preface

The information contained within these pages has helped thousands of people to improve their lives and achieve their dreams; but perhaps one of the most amazing things about this book is that I've managed to write it at all. You see, until the age of twenty-nine I couldn't read or write properly. Then through a bizarre set of circumstances I discovered something that totally changed every aspect of my life.

Allow me to share my story with you. I was born into a travelling funfair family and grew up having homes in three different locations each year: one was on the Isle of Wight where my father operated his summer business, one was the caravan that we travelled around in with the fairs, and the third was near Heathrow Airport where we'd park the caravan for the winter.

With these three different homes came three different sets of friends, three different outlooks on life, at least two (and sometimes three) different schools. The timing of our moves meant that I often turned up at a new school in the middle of mock exams. The teachers generally thought it unfair that I should sit the tests having missed the course-work and, because I would be staying only a few months before moving on again, I would invariably find myself sitting in a temporary class: normally metalwork or woodwork. I often had as many as fifteen periods of metalwork or woodwork a week and became quite good at these things, but I didn't progress in other areas such as reading, writing and arithmetic. I have dyslexia and found spelling particularly difficult. Some teachers made a real effort and my parents paid for private lessons, but I just couldn't get the hang of it.

By the age of fourteen I'd fallen way behind the other kids

and, after pestering my father for some time, he allowed me to leave school. In those days it was the norm for children from fairground families to leave school early and the general attitude was: 'If you can read and write a little, and if you know how many beans make five, that's good enough.' It was time to learn about life.

I thought working full time with my father instead of going to school was great, and in some ways it was, but it was also pretty stupid. There is a saying that goes: 'If you don't use it, you lose it.' I didn't have much ability to read and write in the first place; once I left school and stopped exercising what little skill I had, I lost it completely. By the age of eighteen my ability to read and write was so poor that I couldn't fill out forms, send a postcard, or even write a cheque without help.

However, I was determined that none of this would hold me back in life, and I sought to build on my father's success by expanding the family business. At nineteen I became one of the youngest licensees in the country when I opened a disco. With my brother George's help I built the business, became really successful, and stayed in the club business for twelve years.

Then, in the early 1990s, things changed dramatically. The disco scene gave way to the rave culture, the British economy went into recession, and I made some bad business decisions. In a very short space of time I lost everything: my business, my home, most of my possessions, and finally my marriage fell apart.

I moved back into in my parents' house, 'signed on' with social security, and the family business went into receivership with debts of nearly £1 million. I found this very hard to deal with and fell into a state of depression. There didn't seem much chance of getting back on my feet. The whole family had been left penniless and the threat of eviction hung over my parents' heads as it seemed their home would be repossessed. I had no formal qualifications and no real work experience, so there was nothing of substance that I could put on a CV.

Looking back, I now consider that period as a time of good

fortune. In an effort to make some extra money I joined a sales organization; there I met a man who helped me to change my life. His name was Mike Rosewarne and he was a teacher of personal development. His message was simple: 'If you think you can, you can, if you think you can't you can't – and either way you're right.'

I'd heard the saying several times before, as I expect you have. It's an old truth. But this time I heard it when I was looking for some answers and I listened with an open mind. I felt deeply inspired and uplifted by the notion that I could somehow improve my life through thinking differently. The biggest difference was that Mike put some scientific substance behind the statement that made a lot of sense and gave it real power.

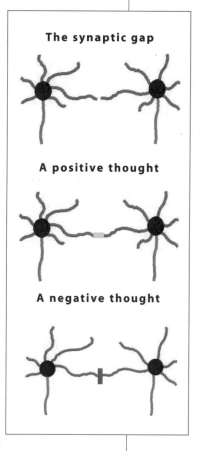

The synaptic gap

A positive thought

A negative thought

I learned that everyone has billions of brain cells with 'arms' called *dendrites*. Each of the dendrites is separated by a slight gap known as the *synaptic gap*. When you have a thought you spark an impulse in the centre (the *nucleus*) of the brain cell that travels along each of the dendrites, seeking to make connection with other dendrites, so that the thought spreads outwards to form a pattern of understanding, or train of thought.

If your thought is positive – whether to do with your self, your life, or situation – the positive impulse triggers the release of a chemical called *serotonin* from the end of the dendrite 'arm'. Serotonin is the chemical that gives you the feeling of happiness and well-being; it also acts as *a conductor* and bridges the synaptic gap, allowing your thought to continue on its journey.

If however the thought you have is negative, it triggers the release of a chemical called *cortisone* instead, which prompts feelings of sadness and depression. It also works as an insulator, effectively blocking or limiting the free-flow of thoughts and ideas.

Thinking '*I can*' releases chemicals and creates brain-cell connections that in turn produce a 'synergy of thought' and the birth of ideas or answers. Thinking '*I can't*' blocks the free-flow of thought, which results only in seeing more of the problem and reasons for giving up altogether.

After a little hesitation and some ego-resistance, because the concept just seemed too simplistic, I made a deal with myself to start thinking 'I can' with everything in my life. I focused most fully on my Main Goal: my belief that I could overcome my dyslexia and learn to read and write well. It took me one year.

I didn't go back to school to achieve my goal and didn't attend night classes. The real key was to build my belief that I could do it and physically to practise whenever possible. Little by little the words came into focus. Within eighteen months I had taught myself to speed-read.

I went through an enormous change. It is hard to describe how wonderful it felt to discover I could *learn* at what seemed such a late age. It gave me hope for the future and a fantastic boost to my self-esteem. Even at a point when the nightclub had been really successful, the truth is that I had always felt inferior to other people in some way. I thought that not being able to read or write properly made other people better than me; that I was less than them.

Gaining the ability was like being given a key that let me out of prison. I developed a passion for reading, a hunger for knowledge, and would read at least a book a week. I felt so grateful for this new gift of reading and writing that I decided to focus my reading in the area that had helped me the most: personal development and self-improvement. I became fascinated with the brain and the mind, and how we can help to develop them in order to maximize our potential.

Everything that I learned I applied to myself and then shared with my friends. Every area of my life started to take off. The easiest area to measure improvement was in my work, where my performance shot up. A lot of people wanted to know what I was doing to make the difference and increasingly I found myself giving presentations.

From there it was a short step to running regular 'personal leadership programmes' where I was able to share the ideas that had made such a difference to my life. In particular, I wanted to share the amazing technique I'd developed that would help people to achieve real magic in life: Goal Mapping.

I now share this powerful way to achieve dreams and ambitions with tens of thousands of people around the world in schools, businesses and groups of the general public.

It is now my great pleasure to share Goal Mapping and the Principles of Success with you. May this book help you to achieve whatever you truly desire.

Wishing you love, light and laughter.

Brian Mayne

Introduction

Learn to set your best intentions towards who you want to be and what you want to achieve, in all the areas of your life, and the world will be yours.

We are all natural-born masters of imagination and creation. Each of us is constantly conjuring up thoughts or creating something. Sometimes we manifest the things we desire, and sometimes the things we dread; sometimes we create consciously, and sometimes unconsciously; but we are always creating something.

The key to personal success and the path to true and lasting happiness is learning the ability to *set* and *hold* a thought that is positive in its intention, so as to develop your conscious desires, rather than your unconscious fears.

> The Universe has no choice but to bring you the direct manifestation of your thought about it.
> **NEALE DONALD WALSCH**

In every generation and in every culture there has always been a small minority of people who have understood and applied the natural principles of creation to manifest their desires. Any book on success from any area of the world will contain a section on goal-setting, intention setting, conscious manifestation, or its equivalent. The principles are included in the most ancient wisdom.

Although this timeless wisdom of how to turn *thoughts into things* has never been a secret, it is by its very nature *hidden* or obscured from our everyday view, and must therefore be sought out and revealed to each person who strives for success.

> The aspects of things that are most important to us are hidden because of their simplicity and familiarity.
> **LUDWIG WITTGENSTEIN**

Two Indian saints sat watching a crowded bazaar. One turned to the other and said: 'See here in the crowd. All have got rupees in their bundle, but how to undo the knot, that they do not know, and therefore are they paupers.'

One of the greatest realizations in my own life came at a time when I had lost almost everything: that I, just like everybody else in the world, was already successful beyond measure. All I needed to do was figure out the mental and emotional combination that would allow me to unlock my potential, thereby enabling me to create more of what I consciously wanted, and less of what I didn't want.

The Nature of Success

The universe and everything in it is a success, and that includes YOU.

> If we all did the things that we are capable of doing we would literally astound ourselves.
> **THOMAS EDISON**
>
> Ask and you will receive. Seek and you will find. Knock and the door will be opened to you.
> **MATTHEW 7:7**

Success is the natural result of the laws and principles that govern the process of creation. All of life itself is a success, and perhaps the greatest success of all is the continuous unfolding of the universe, where every living entity can be deemed 'a winner'.

As humans, we tend to define success not so much in relation to our life or physical existence, which so many people take for granted, but in relation to the achievement of our individual and material desires or wishes: the specific things we want.

What does being successful mean to you? Does it mean being financially successful, having a fulfilling career, a beautiful home, a car, a boat, or going on amazing holidays? Or does it mean having a wonderful family, great friends, or a romantic relationship? Maybe it means being thought of highly by friends, family and colleagues.

Success means different things to different people at different times, and there are probably as many varied definitions of success as there are people who want to be successful.

I believe that true success depends upon achieving a balance of just three core values: happiness, peace of mind, and an experience of abundance. After all, what everybody wants ultimately is happiness, peace and plenty, regardless of the particular path their life may take.

Abundance or plenty, like success itself, will be relative to each person. In essence it means simply that you have 'enough'. What might be enough for me may not be enough for you, or vice versa, but as long as you have enough it means you are not in want.

You do not need necessarily to be rich to be in abundance. It is not so much a physical quantity as a mental outlook. Some of my friends would appear on paper to have precious little if you were to add up their material wealth, however, they have enough for the way they have chosen to live their life; they also have peace of mind and happiness. I class them as truly successful.

In contrast, other people may be fabulously wealthy but desperately miserable and their material successes have come to mean little to them. No matter what you may achieve in your life, without happiness and a sense of peace it will soon start to lose its flavour and become unfulfilling. Being happy, like living with peace of mind or achieving abundance, is a quality that needs to be studied, learnt, worked for and mastered.

> Happiness is not an accident. Nor is it something you wish for. Happiness is something you design.
> **JIM ROHN**

> He who knows much about others may be learned, but he who understands himself is more intelligent. He who controls others may be powerful, but he who has mastered himself is mightier still.
> **LAO-TSU**

Success is on Purpose

Lasting success is never an accident – it's on purpose. It is the natural result of taking successful actions and thinking successful thoughts.

I've often heard it argued that people who achieve true and lasting success, happiness, peace and abundance, have just been lucky in some way: they were born into the right family, got the right start, had a good education, made the right contacts that led to a great job or career. I'll agree that any of the aforementioned can be a definite advantage, but the fact remains that if you study history you'll find many great names shining forth who had the worst possible start:

> **Wealth is the product of a man's ability to think.**
> **AYN RAND**
>
> **Most people search high and wide for the keys to success. If they only knew, the key to their dreams lies within.**
> **GEORGE WASHINGTON CARVER**

◆ Abraham Lincoln was born into absolute poverty and only ever received three months' formal education in his entire life. He overcame huge challenges to become one of the greatest presidents of America.

◆ Thomas Edison was the most prolific inventor of the twentieth century. He received three months' formal education and no scientific training, but went on to patent over 1,200 different inventions.

◆ Anita Roddick, founder of Body Shop, the high street chain, needed to borrow money from friends to start her business, which is now valued at tens of millions of pounds.

There are countless thousands of others who start with nothing and through pure intention and effort, create something. In contrast, pick up a newspaper, turn on the television or listen to the radio and you will discover the latest story of someone who was born into total privilege, started with all the financial and material advantages, but failed to learn the critical lessons of success and ultimately it cost them everything.

What all of this tells us is that success is not an accident; success happens for a reason. Success is *on purpose*. Many people argue that a big part of success is luck, just as winning the lottery is; but luck relates to momentary success, whereas true success is not static, it's constantly on the move like a flowing river. If the lottery winner does not learn the lessons of success it will be only a short time before he or she is parted from their winnings. It's amazing how many people who come into good fortune do not learn the lessons of success, and actually end up worse off.

The most important thing to understand about success, and what I find so inspiring, is that lasting success happens for a reason. That means it has a formula: a formula that can be studied, learned, repeated and enjoyed by anyone who truly desires to achieve something.

> **The greatest discovery of my generation is that man can alter his life simply by altering his attitude of mind.**
> **WILLIAM JAMES**

The Laws of Success

Learning the natural laws of creation and living in harmony with them, is like cracking the combination that will unlock the treasure chest of your potential.

We live in a physical world that is governed by fundamental laws, such as the law of gravity and the law of motion. Chief amongst all these laws is the law of cause and effect, which states simply that there are no accidents. Things that happen in the world are the *effects*, which are created or triggered by specific *causes*.

When we apply the law of cause and effect to our lives it dictates that the situations we experience – the *effects* – are most often *caused* or influenced by our actions and behaviour. If we continue to follow

> **The process of creation starts with thought – an idea, conception, visualization. Everything you see was once someone's idea. Nothing exists in your world that did not first exist as pure thought.**
> **NEALE DONALD WALSCH**

this chain backwards, the ultimate *cause* is our thoughts.

Successful people think successful thoughts. This means they are constantly setting successful *causes* in motion, which, like seeds, grow eventually into successful *effects* or results, whether within their relationships, their career, or life generally. Successful people think about succeeding. They develop a success mindset where even failure is viewed as part of the process of achieving long-term success.

When Thomas Edison was trying to perfect the electric light bulb he was already famous for other inventions. A reporter came to interview him one day and remarked: 'Mr Edison, you have failed over 5,000 times in your efforts to invent electric light, won't you now give up this folly?' Edison replied, 'Young man, you don't understand the way the world works. I have not failed 5,000 times. I have successfully identified 5,000 ways that will not work, and that puts me 5,000 ways closer to the way that will work.' It took Thomas Edison over 10,000 experiments to create the carbon-impregnated filament that still forms the basis of our lighting industry today.

> **I am not discouraged, because every wrong attempt discarded is another step forward.**
> **THOMAS EDISON**

Failing to Succeed

Everyone experiences failure at some point in life, and successful people experience it more than most.

One of the great differences between successful and unsuccessful people is that successful people have learnt a major life lesson and do not see failure as a negative dead end that stops them in their tracks. Instead they see it as a learning opportunity, a signpost that helps point out the right path forward.

There are certain things in life that you can learn to get right only by getting them wrong first. This is one of the natural learning strategies that we are all

> **Failure is, in a sense, the highway to success.**
> **JOHN KEATS**

born with; it's called 'trial and error'. During the months that I watched my baby daughter learning to walk she fell over many times in her efforts, but at no point did she view her falls as failure and give up. She understood at a subconscious level that falling was part of the process of her mastering the skill of walking.

As adults we tend to lose sight of this important lesson and instead become overwhelmed by our negative emotions and sometimes even develop a fear of failure. The social viewpoint of the majority is that failure is negative or bad, and that failure makes you a bad person in some way.

I first noticed this fear of failure in myself when I was seventeen and about to take my driving test. The night before my exam I told all my mates that I would be taking them out cruising in the car the next day. But I didn't pass, and later had to face their laughter and teasing about failing. The second time I took my test I did exactly the same thing – again telling my friends that I would pick them up in the car later. I didn't pass that test either. This time their laughter was louder and the emotional pain that I felt was greater. The third time I took my test I didn't tell a soul, because I didn't want to go through the pain of feeling like a failure and facing more ridicule.

I did pass my third test and, looking back on it now, I can see that the experience gained from the first two so-called 'failures' helped me ultimately to succeed in my third attempt.

Often the stigma of failure is so strong that it leads people to blame the situation instead of looking at themselves and accepting that they could have done things differently. This prevents them from seeing their experience and themselves clearly and thereby stops them learning from it. This in turn may result in them repeating their mistakes later in life.

Typically, people try something once and if it doesn't work

> A smooth sea never made a skilled mariner.
> **OLD ENGLISH PROVERB**

> The measure of success is not whether you have a tough problem to deal with, but whether it's the same problem you had last year.
> **JOHN FOSTER DULLES**

> Failure equals a few errors in judgement, repeated every day.
> **JIM RHON**

may try a second time. Not as many try for a third time, and most of those who do don't tell anyone about it in case they should fail. In general, people become disillusioned or distracted by their perceived limitations and setbacks. Often it takes a long time for them to learn the lesson in defeat, to regain their motivation, and focus once more on their intended direction. Multiply this process of slow growth by the number of lessons that need to be learnt for a truly successful life, and the time span becomes enormous.

There is an ancient expression: 'Too soon old, too late smart.' By the time most people have figured out how to run their lives successfully, they feel as though the life is running out of them. Some people become so paralyzed by the fear of failure that it prevents them from attempting anything new at all. These people retreat slowly into a shrinking comfort zone of stagnation and ever-reducing cycles of justification.

> You don't fail when you fall, you fail when you refuse to get up.
> **ANON**

> If youth knew, if age could.
> **HENRI ESTIENNE**

In contrast, truly successful people, while not always successful in every attempt, view any failure as a lesson to be learnt, a character flaw to be corrected, or a pitfall to avoid for the future. Failure is neither negative nor permanent in the eyes of a successful person, it is always seen as providing valuable information that points to future success. So long as you learn from it and have another go failure is only ever fleeting; it's giving up that makes it permanent.

All in The Mind

If you think you can, you can. If you think you can't, you can't, and either way you'll prove yourself right.

Whether you see failure as a stumbling block or stepping-stone will depend upon how you use you mind. It is perhaps our greatest human freedom that each of us, no matter what our physical situation, is always free and able to choose our thoughts.

Each of your thoughts is a *cause* set in motion that triggers an *effect*. The thoughts that you repeat most often gradually become your *dominant thoughts*, which are eventually accepted as *true* by your subconscious. These become *habitual thoughts*, and therefore automatic. In short they become your *beliefs*.

A belief of any nature represents an automatic way of thinking that has been developed in response, or in reaction, to a given situation or stimulus. Sometimes your beliefs will be positive and serve you, and sometimes they will be negative and limit you. Whether positive or negative they will *always* be true for you if you accept them without question.

When I was growing up I developed and held the limiting belief that I'd never be able to read or write well because of my dyslexia, and my belief sustained and perpetuated that reality. Not until I was an adult and learnt about the power of positive thinking and its link with beliefs, did I question my self-limiting outlook and replace it with a positive empowering belief. At that point I took the first step on a journey to overcome my dyslexia.

What was particularly important in helping me to achieve this, and all other goals since, was learning about the workings of my subconscious mind and how I could condition it for success through setting goals.

> We are what we think. All that we are arises with our thoughts. With our thoughts we make our world.
> **THE BUDDHA**

> Every time we think, every time we feel, every time we exercise our will, we are sowing.
> **KENNETH COPELAND**

> As thou hast believed, so be it done unto thee.
> **MATTHEW 8.13**

Your Amazing Subconscious

Your subconscious mind is like the most amazing servant, waiting to act on the goal or command from your conscious mind.

Imagine that your brain is like a computer. Your conscious mind could be compared to the front screen whilst your subconscious mind is like the internal control programs that are not seen directly. Both your conscious and your subconscious drive what you see through the screen.

New discoveries about how the mind works are being made on an almost daily basis. It is now known for certain that the subconscious mind is extremely powerful. It has the capacity to do things that doctors and scientists still don't fully understand, and which most people will never properly utilize. Your subconscious works non-stop, twenty-four hours a day, whether you are awake or asleep. Its main functions are to keep you well and healthy and to serve your every need.

Together your conscious and subconscious form a unique partnership. Your conscious mind is like the captain of a ship and has the responsibility for setting the direction and giving the commands, and your subconscious is like the crew that must obey the captain's orders.

However, for all its enormous power there is one crucial function that your subconscious cannot perform – it cannot question or make *value judgements*. That is, it can't determine whether something is right or wrong for you, good or bad for you, true or false. That task remains the responsibility of your *questioning* conscious mind.

> They can because they think they can.
> **VIRGIL**
>
> Your own mind is a sacred enclosure into which nothing harmful can enter except by your permission
> **RALPH WALDO EMERSON**

Commanding the Crew

Your subconscious thoughts will follow your direction.

The prime way in which your conscious captain communicates with your subconscious crew is through the thoughts that you think. Every thought is a goal or command for your subconscious to obey. The thoughts you repeat most often, and those connected to the strongest emotions, become your *dominant thoughts* and the priority commands that your subconscious obeys.

Have you ever had the experience of getting in your car, deciding to drive somewhere, and then finding that you've arrived without being able to remember much of the journey? This common experience is made possible because when you think about going to your chosen destination, your subconscious obeys your command, while your conscious mind ponders other things during the journey. In fact your subconscious instructs ninety per cent of all your driving or *doing* in all areas of your life and daily activities.

The majority of people rarely stop to think about this too deeply, instead they take it for granted and go through life on a sort of subconscious autopilot. However, it is vitally important to understand that your subconscious is designed like a guided missile system and always seeks a target. If you are not giving your subconscious crew conscious and clearly defined commands about where you want to go in life, it will simply select your *dominant thought* as the target and act on that by default.

Returning again to a driving scenario – perhaps like so many other people, you have had the experience of getting in your car to drive somewhere without clearly thinking about or picturing your intended destination. As a result, instead of taking the turn you needed, your subconscious followed an old and *dominant* route instruction that was still strong in your memory. While this is irritating and time wasting, far more detrimental for many people is that their consistent and *dominant thoughts* will not be of the positive things they want to achieve, they will often be the things they *fear*.

If you focus regularly on what you don't want: like not having enough money to pay your bills, or breaking up with your loved one, or becoming ill, or losing your temper, your subconscious, unable to make value judgements, will simply accept the picture

> The mind is the limit. As long as the mind can envision the fact that you can do something, you can do it – as long as you really believe a 100 per cent.
>
> **ARNOLD SCHWARZENEGGER**

> Our doubts are traitors, and make us lose the good we oft might win, by fearing to attempt.
>
> **WILLIAM SHAKESPEARE**

> Concerning all acts of initiative and creation, there is one elementary truth – that the moment one definitely commits oneself, then Providence moves too.
>
> **W.H. MURRAY**

> ⟩ People with goals succeed because they know where they are going... It's as simple as that. ✕
>
> **EARL NIGHTINGALE**

in your thoughts as the goal or target to be achieved and will start working to pursue it. Repeated negative thoughts cause your subconscious to send you into a form of self-sabotage. The majority of people diminish their power greatly by spending mental and emotional energy thinking about failing.

A major distinction between people who see themselves as successful and people who consider themselves to be unsuccessful is that successful people stay fully focused on what they *want* and generate great personal power, rather than allowing themselves to become distracted and deflated by worrying about what they fear.

The Art of Goal-setting

Hold the thought of what you want by turning it into a goal.

Every achievement of any nature, whether great or small, is always preceded by a goal. Goal-setting is the master art or skill for life because it is the ability that enables us to gain all other skills and abilities.

Each of us is a natural-born goal-setter. Goal-setting is, quite simply, the main function of our mind. Our conscious mind sets the goal via a thought and our subconscious obeys by working to achieve it. Successful people learn, either consciously or unconsciously, to develop this natural mental ability into a powerful tool for personal achievement.

History shows us that all sorts of people achieve all manner of amazing things when they learn to focus their mind, harness their motivation and stay committed to their vision through purposeful action. The key technique or strategy for achieving this state of mind and way of being is goal-setting.

Before Hannibal crossed the Alps in 218 BC he set the goal to do so; before Einstein discovered the theory of relativity he set the goal to look for it; before a great artist creates any form of masterpiece, the goal is first set in their mind.

Enhancing your ability to set goals correctly is fundamental to your future success in life. Conscious goal-setting is a simple but profound mind-set and a way of thinking. Goal-setting is not just a formula, it's a system of disciplines that forms a habit that, with time, crystallizes into an attitude to life.

> I dream my painting and then paint my dream.
> **VINCENT VAN GOGH**

Many people will be aware of the idea of setting goals and some will have tried conscious goal-setting in the past. But very few people will have developed the art of setting goals correctly or will be aware of the natural and psychological reasons as to why goal-setting works.

The Yale University Survey

In 1953 a survey was conducted with the graduating class at Yale University. The results showed that only 4 per cent of the class had set clearly written goals for their future. Twenty years later, in 1973, the surviving members of the class of '53 were interviewed again. It was discovered that the 4 per cent who had set goals were worth more in financial terms (that being the easiest value to measure) than the other 96 per cent added together.

> Climb high; Climb far.
> Your goal the sky;
> Your aim the star.
> **INSCRIPTION AT WILLIAMS COLLEGE**

Sadly, only around 3–4 per cent of the general population, regardless of background, set regular written goals. It's likely to be no coincidence that 95 per cent of the population (almost the same percentage as those who don't set goals) retire dependent on others: whether that means dependence upon family, friends, charity, company or state pension. Only 5 per cent of the population retires with sufficient personal resources to be able to provide for themselves. About 2 per cent are those who receive inherited wealth, the other 3–4 per cent are self-made people –

the ones who set regular, conscious goals.

Please don't make the mistake of thinking that goal-setting is something reserved only for material or financial gain. Goal-setting is the natural way for our mind to work, which means that every area and aspect of our lives needs to be goal-orientated if we are to reach our full potential and live our best life.

Every time you think a thought and make a decision to do something you are setting a goal. Saying, 'I'll finish the job and then I'll have a break' or, 'I'll just do the housework and then have a coffee' are examples of natural goal-setting. It's the process of making a conscious decision, setting a target and, if necessary, delaying gratification until the target has been achieved. Getting up this morning was a goal that you achieved. Going to work, school or staying at home is a goal. To read this book is a goal. As mentioned earlier, any thought you have consistently becomes by default a goal for your subconscious to obey.

> Plan for the future, because that is where you are going to spend the rest of your life.
>
> **MARK TWAIN**

> The most important thing about goals is having one.
>
> **GEOFFRY F. ABERT**

Achieving your goal is not necessarily the most important element of the goal-setting process; it's having one in the first place that brings the greatest benefit. Having a reason to get out of bed in the morning and make an effort is a major aspect in making the experience of life worthwhile. To pursue a goal will require you invariably to grow in some way as a person. It's this growth – the being 'you' at your best – that results ultimately in creating your best experiences.

One of the first books I was able to read properly was *Psycho-Cybernetics* by Maxwell Maltz. In it he says something very profound: 'Emotionally we are designed like a bicycle – if we are not moving towards something, we lose our equilibrium or balance and fall over.'

There will always be rocks in the road of life; they are simply part of the journey. If you keep up some momentum while riding your bike, though the ride may get a little bumpy, you'll get over the rocks one way or another. However, if you have no momentum in your life, there is nothing that you're aiming for, and no compelling reason for being, then the slightest pebble of upset will be enough to topple you from your saddle and send you crashing to the ground. Having a goal is equivalent to having a target and a motive – it gives you motivation and helps you retain your balance and keep your momentum.

> You must have courage to bet on your ideals, to take calculated risk, and act. Everyday living requires courage if life is to be effective and bring happiness.
>
> **MAXWELL MALTZ**

Think of a Picture

We all think in pictures, as well as in words.

My awareness of this ongoing process was given a great boost by discovering the technique of Goal Mapping. I use the term *discovering* purposefully because I don't see myself as its inventor. Goal Mapping came into my mind fully formed, in a single instant. My flash of insight occurred late one night while driving my car, I had been asking myself with some intensity: 'Why are some people so much more successful than others?'

Although I envisioned the entire technique in a single flash, it took me nearly a year to get that momentary insight recorded onto paper in the form of a training programme, and even longer to understand why the technique worked so well in helping people achieve their dreams.

One of the main aspects and power sources of the Goal Mapping technique is its mirrored structure of words and pictures. We each have two sides to our brain. Our left-brain is generally logical, analytical, mathematical, and thinks by using words; whereas our right-brain is emotional, lateral, intuitive, and thinks by using pictures. To create maximum power in your goal-setting requires setting your intentions in both thought and feeling.

> The secret to productive goal - setting is in establishing clearly defined goals, writing them down and then focusing on them several times a day with words, pictures and emotions as if we've already achieved them.
>
> **DENIS WAITLEY**

The Technique of Goal Mapping

Ancient wisdom, combined with scientific under-standing, creates real power.

The techniques of goal-setting have evolved over many years and are derived from esoteric and secretive doctrines. They were taught originally only to a privileged few – because they promoted the concept of self-determination and conscious development. The principles have since become integrated into a range of self-help systems that are available worldwide and used by the masses. Each new goal-setting formula attempts to be more effective and powerful than the last. As man's knowledge of the workings of the mind has advanced, so too the effectiveness and power of various goal-setting programmes has increased.

However, regardless of individual detail, the central effectiveness of any goal-setting technique lies in its facility to connect your consciously chosen goals to your subconscious mind, in a way that is sufficiently powerful for your subconscious to accept your goal as the *dominant command* to be pursued.

Traditionally, the typical method of 'drumming in' this subconscious acceptance of facts and goals (particularly in schools) has been through repetition, usually involving the process of writing and re-writing the goal again and again, line after line, hundreds of times each day. This method does work for some people, but most find it too boring, too time consuming, and largely ineffective. The great majority give up long before their subconscious has received the new dominant command or goal. One of the challenges of this approach is that it caters predominantly for the left-brain, which has a limited path to the subconscious mind.

However, in recent years there have been tremendous break-throughs in understanding about how we learn. These have

> No army can withstand the strength of an idea whose time has come.
>
> **Victor Hugo**
>
> You, too, can determine what you want. You can decide on your major objectives, targets, aims, and destination.
>
> **W. Clement Stone**

shown clearly what ancient teachings always knew: that the major pathway to the subconscious lies not through the left side of the brain, which thinks in words, but through the right side of the brain, which thinks in pictures.

The technique of Goal Mapping uses a unique combination of words and pictures to activate both the left- and right-brain in order to create maximum connection to the subconscious at a deep level; thereby powerfully imbedding any consciously-desired goals.

Based on proven principles of traditional goal-setting combined with the power of cutting-edge learning strategies, Goal Mapping stimulates whole-brain activity and harnesses the intrinsic aspects necessary for any kind of conscious, intended success.

The seven steps of Goal Mapping will guide you to success through consideration of *what, why, when, how, and who* will move you forwards. Goal Mapping takes each person through the process of identifying their goals, defining their motives and committing to taking action. (See Chapter 6.) A personalized 'Goal Map' captures this empowering information in both words and pictures, thereby communicating it clearly to the user's subconscious autopilot. Your completed Goal Map becomes the blueprint for your future success.

Whether or not you know what you want out of life, if you know that you want something different and want to bring your future into focus, continue with me now as we begin our journey into the creativity, logic and clarity of Goal Mapping.

> We are what and where we are because we have first imagined it.
>
> **DONALD CURTIS**

> So – do you want your life to 'take off'? Begin at once to imagine it the way you want it to be – and move into that. Check every thought, word and action that does not fall into harmony with that. Move away from those.
>
> **NEALE DONALD WALSCH**

How to Get The Best From This Book

The pages that follow form an instruction manual for achievement and explain a universal philosophy of success that is based on natural law and motivational psychology; the foundations on which the technique of Goal Mapping is built. The seven steps of Goal Mapping (Chapter 6) are designed as a complete and self-contained system for achieving success but have been designed to work in alignment with natural and universal laws of manifestation (Chapter 4).

I recommend initially that you read the entire book complete the exercises and create your first Goal Map, so as to understand fully the Goal Mapping technique and supporting philosophy. Then afterwards create some space and time during which you can create another Goal Map incorporating any new insights or developments. Because success and Goal Mapping are ongoing I also recommend that you update your Goal Map regularly and create additional ones whenever you are seeking to achieve anything new. In this way you will transform your Goal Mapping ability gradually from a learned skill in to an internalized habit or approach to life.

> Nothing can stop the man with the right mental attitude from achieving his goal: Nothing on earth can help the man with the wrong mental attitude.
>
> **THOMAS JEFFERSON**

Preparing for your inner journey

Before you embark any further on your journey to create your Goal Map I have one simple but important request that will help you achieve optimum progress: create a little *possibility consciousness* in your mind.

Possibility Consciousness

Our conscious minds are always questioning and evaluating, filtering information through our current viewpoints and beliefs. While this is a great benefit in life generally, it can also be a huge drawback, because if you prejudge the information you are receiving and decide that it is of no real relevance, you will filter out sections of value and may miss something of great importance.

I therefore request that you create a space in your mind for *possibility* and place all the information, ideas, principles and concepts that you are about to learn into this space. Then once you reach the end of the book, you will be in an informed position to evaluate how the information, and the Goal Mapping technique itself, will best serve you. Have fun on your journey.

> A little knowledge is a dangerous thing. Drink deep, or taste not the Pierian spring. There shallow draughts intoxicate the brain, and drinking largely sobers us again.
> **ALEXANDER POPE**

Part One

The Principles
of Success

Chapter 1

Life's a Goal

All of life has a goal – it's the drive of evolution, the urge to grow and become more.

Everything within creation, whether animal, mineral or vegetable, has the natural urge to survive, move forwards and thrive. It is our intrinsic purpose and built-in goal. The goal is known as evolution and is pre-set in animals, driven by instinct: a need to survive. But humans have more than instinct, we have intellect and intuition, and determine our own thinking, habits and actions, which means we are free to select the evolutionary *goal* for ourselves.

Everything in the universe is in the process of evolution and is therefore goal-orientated towards survival. The goal of nature and the drive of evolution have always been to move forwards by gathering particles, atoms and molecules together and organizing them into higher, more sophisticated, and complex structures and life forms. Nature's ongoing goal is to develop and expand: from an individual atom to an entire solar system, from the amoeba with its single cell to a zebra with billions of cells.

> I know of no more encouraging fact than the unquestioning ability of man to elevate his life by a conscious endeavour.
> **HENRY DAVID THOREAU**

Mankind is also a part of nature, which means that this primeval impulse of evolutionary change is present within every one of us. The natural desire to move forwards, grow and thrive is woven into the very fabric of our being. From the moment we enter the world this driving force is at work and it feeds the spring in our step and our urge to explore. The great difference between us and all other life that feels this force is that we have the free will to select the direction of the evolutionary drive.

Treasure the Gift

We are conscious co-creators of our own creation – our free will is a reflection of our divinity.

I believe our greatest gift is that we are each personally *response-able* – able to choose our own response in life – and therefore free to select our own goals, set our own direction and define our own purpose.

Yet so often I meet people who neglect this great gift, this divine right. They range from those who have never taken the time to sit down and think about what they really want, to those who don't believe they have personal power or control over their life and circumstances. Many people seem afraid, or even disgusted, at the idea of setting goals, perhaps due to distorted beliefs that money and material success are wrong in some way, or that it's 'unspiritual' to prosper too much. Occasionally I meet people who fear any form of wealth or abundance at all. However, I rarely meet anyone who consciously wants to be worse off than they are right now.

The feeling of moving backwards in your life is akin to a feeling of mental and emotional breakdown, of physical decline or

> We were born to make manifest the glory of God that is within us. It is not just in some of us; it is in everyone.
> **MARIANNE WILLIAMSON**

> We are co-creators with God, not puppets on a string waiting for something to happen.
> **LEO BOOTH**

fatigue. It's opposite to the drive of life and evolution. As Tony Wilson, a great speaker and a good friend of mine, says: 'There are only two true states in nature, *green and growing* or *ripe and rotten*, choose which you wish to be.'

In my experience, everyone in their right mind wants to feel they are 'green and growing'; making progress and better off today than they were last year. This may not be in terms of financial or material gain, but perhaps due to a new skill learned or some new knowledge acquired. Achievements such as gaining a qualification, passing a test, profoundly developing some aspect of themselves (such as becoming more patient, caring, understanding, determined, motivated, focused) or whatever is most important to them.

All the above, just like any other type of achievement – such as being happy, content, or spiritually aware – are created through setting a goal or intention. Quite simply the act of goal-setting is in harmony with, and aligned to, the natural drive of life: it's all about *moving forwards*. As Abraham Maslow stated at the beginning of the twentieth century: 'Man is only truly happy when he feels that he is making progress and becoming more.'

> **Happiness is a conscious choice, not an automatic response.**
> **MICHAEL BARTEL**

> **It is the mind that make good or ill, that make wretch or happy, rich or poor.**
> **EDMUND SPENSER**

Throughout history the evolutionary journey of humanity has been one long line of goals. Some people may feel that this has led us to a place that is not looking too good. I'd be the first to agree that there are many things we need to change if the planet and life upon it are to flourish long-term; but it's pointless to blame goal-setting for the poverty, the pollution, the poisoning of our land or for the mess we're in. Progress through goal-setting is in our nature; it's the way our minds have evolved. To bring about positive evolutionary change we need simply to change the focus of our intentions and the goals that we pursue.

Conscious Goal-setting

Goal-setting is the major difference that makes the difference.

The fact that goal-setting, or making a conscious decision, is vital to all forms of success has always been understood by those who study and strive for personal improvement and achievement in their life. Study the biography of anyone who has accomplished anything of genuine value and you will discover that they were an avid goal-setter. Open any book on how to live a more successful and fulfilling life and it will contain a section on goal-setting. Talk to the men and women who have reached the top of their chosen profession and they will tell you about the goals they strived for that have helped them to get there.

It's a fact that all high achieving men and women set regular goals and have a clear sense of purpose; they need a high point to aim at, something that makes life worth getting up for. Goal-setting is the main ingredient in any recipe for success.

Occasionally I meet people who hold the view that goal-setting is the reserve only of those wanting to fast-track their career or increase their wealth; but the reality is that more people than ever are setting goals consciously to improve every of aspect of themselves, their lives and their environment.

Goals are the sparks that light the fire of our intention. They are the fuel that keeps our dreams alive, the determining factor that makes the difference between surrender and persistence. For millions of people personal goals represent the turning point that took them from poverty to prosperity, from resignation to resilience and from depression to happiness.

A couple of years ago I saw a friend become completely empowered when he left his corporate job and set a personal goal

> There is only one success – to be able to spend your life in your own way.
> **CHRISTOPHER MORLEY**
>
> There are two things to aim for in life. First to get what you want, and after that, to enjoy it.
> **LOGAN PEARSALL SMITH**

to do something for the environment by reducing landfill. The organization he founded (Green Standards) has so far achieved the diversion of hundreds of tonnes of corporate desks, chairs, and IT equipment away from landfill sites. Instead the office equipment is reconditioned and given a new lease of life in the third world.

More people than ever are becoming philanthropically driven and set goals to help charities, raise funds, and run sponsored marathons. Increasing numbers are setting goals to take early retirement, downgrade their career, and have an exit plan into some form of self-sufficiency. Year on year, a growing tide of people set goals to get fitter, lose weight, stop smoking, lower their cholesterol, de-tox and cleanse. All show examples of positive goal-setting.

> Life is mostly froth and bubbles. Two things stand like stone. Kindness in another's trouble, Courage in your own.
>
> **ADAM LINDSAY GORDON**

> There are no great people in this world, only great challenges which ordinary people rise to meet.
>
> **WILLIAM FREDERICK HALSEY, JR**

Some years ago I met an amazing woman who has since become a great friend and teacher to me. A while before meeting her she had been diagnosed with terminal cancer and given only a few months to live. Although she was devastated at first, and felt like surrendering to fate, her family strongly encouraged her to fight the illness. She told me that the turning point came when she set a clear compelling goal to return to full health and then started looking for treatments that could help her achieve it. That was over fourteen years ago. The illness went into remission and she has enjoyed good health ever since.

Why Goal-setting Works

When you are pursuing something great, it draws out your own personal greatness.

Contained within the character of each individual is the equivalent of a *High Self*, and a *Low Self*. Our High Self represents all of our positive qualities such as: self-motivation, inspiration, responsibility, self-belief and confidence. These are the qualities that ultimately produce successful results in our selves and our lives, even in the face of failure.

On the other hand our Low Self is the opposite of our High Self and has negative character traits such as: procrastination, apathy, blame, defeatism, self-doubt, and insecurity. Our Low Self represents us at our worst and the characteristics result invariably in some form of failure, even in the light of success: for instance, when we are presented with a positive opportunity but are unable to muster the confidence or motivation to seize it.

Life is continuous change and can trigger a roller-coaster ride of emotional ups and downs, attitudes and reactions. Sometimes our responses will be positive and come from our High Self. At other times they can be negative and stem from our Low Self. But because we are all creatures of habit, whichever aspect of our Self we engage in the most, whether High or Low, will gradually become dominant. Our most common response is reinforced and becomes the automatic or regular response to the situations that arise.

The universal law of cause and effect dictates that negative actions and re-actions create ultimately negative results; while positive actions or re-actions create more positive results. Everyone has the ability to create more positive results in their life, regardless of past experience or current circumstance, simply by choosing to approach life from their High Self.

Every time you set a positive goal or think about a positive goal – especially when you commit a goal to

> What we do not see, what most of us never suspect of existing, is the silent but irresistible power which comes to the rescue of those who fight on in the face of discouragement.
>
> **NAPOLEON HILL**

paper – you come from your High Self and activate your success mechanism, which overrides any negative thoughts, attitudes and habits.

Goal-setting is the trigger that fires your imagination and releases your potential. The more you engage in the practise of setting a positive goal, the stronger your connection with your High Self grows and the greater becomes your habit of approaching life with the positive qualities of character that create success. You become energized, activated, and focused.

Many people have positive *intentions* about their future, but intentions can be fleeting thoughts and are not focused goals. We need to find a way of holding onto them, to clarify our goals and stay mindful of what we deem important. So many good intentions and valuable insights become lost in the busy rush of daily activity and our ever-flowing stream of consciousness.

> **The discipline of writing something down is the first step toward making it happen.**
> LEE IACOCCA

A thought captured on paper and reviewed regularly is held as a goal for your subconscious to pursue; it moves it to another level of power. Like a magnet the thought starts to attract the various elements required for the goal to be achieved.

Goethe put it beautifully:

'Until one is committed there is the chance to draw back; always ineffectiveness. Concerning all acts of initiative and creation there is one elementary truth, the ignorance of which kills countless splendid plans; that the moment one definitely commits oneself, then providence moves too. All sorts of things occur to help one that would not otherwise have occurred. A whole stream of events issues from the decision, raising in one's favour all manner of unforeseen incidents and meetings and material assistance which no man could have dreamed would come his way. Whatever you can do, or dream you can, begin it! Boldness has genius, magic and power in it. Begin it now!'

Your Personal Autopilot

Learn to condition your subconscious for success and you will achieve untold wonders.

One of the most important aspects of goal-setting, and the reason it works, is the nature and working of your subconscious mind. It is a vital point to understand for goal success. As we move through life, facing the situations that come our way on a daily basis, we are generally unaware that it is our subconscious mind that is driving most of our activity, allowing us to take much of what comes our way in our stride, with minimal conscious effort.

Although the subconscious mind does most of the work, the conscious mind has the *responsibility* of choosing the direction or target – for example, tying your shoelaces is quite a complex process, but once mastered, the technique becomes an automatic sub-conscious activity. We need only to think consciously about what we want to set the process in motion. The conscious / subconscious partnership is a useful one that has served humankind throughout history. The process of consciously choosing or deciding, then subconsciously doing or acting, is natural to the way that our mind has evolved, and when used properly can help us to achieve our every aim.

Your subconscious is so powerful that it can perform complex equations in milliseconds; for example, when accurately estimating the speed of an oncoming car as you cross a busy road and assessing how long it will take you to reach the other side; or when tracking the speed and direction of a moving ball as you jump and effortlessly pluck it from the air.

> The ability to discipline yourself to delay gratification in the short term in order to enjoy greater rewards in the long term is the indispensable prerequisite for success.
> **BRIAN TRACY**

> Goals are new, forward-moving objectives. They magnetize you towards them.
> **MARK VICTOR HANSEN**

My Mental Alarm Clock

Did you know that no-one really needs an alarm clock? Have you ever had the experience of wanting to be up really early for something that is so crucial that you set two alarms *plus* arrange an early morning call? Then, just a few moments before they all go off, you're suddenly wide awake.

When I was about seven years old my uncle said to me, 'Brian, if you tap your head seven times, you'll wake up at 7 o' clock in the morning.' I was just a small child, excited at the idea of learning something new, and I believed my uncle without question. I tried it, it worked like magic, and I've used the method for years.

When I grew older and started to understand how my subconscious works, I realized that the result had been achieved by setting a target or goal for my subconscious to follow. While I still use the technique, I don't bother tapping my head any more. Instead I simply picture the hands of a clock pointing to the time I want to get up, and my belief guarantees that I will wake up within a few moments of that time. What's more, because I'm telling myself to wake from the inside, rather than being *alarmed* from the outside, I wake up feeling much refreshed and energized.

In a similar manner, many people have the experience of going to bed with an unresolved problem or question on their mind, only to wake up in the morning with the answer. A common example of this kind of subconscious goal function is the experience of trying to remember someone's name; although it's 'on the tip of your tongue' you can't quite get it. Then later, usually when you are doing something completely different and have let go of the conscious thought, your subconscious simply releases the name of the person into your mind.

All of the above, and so much more besides, are made possible because your subconscious mind is

> Chance favours the prepared mind.
> **Louis Pasteur**

> Fixing your objective is like identifying the North Star – you sight your compass on it and then use it as the means of getting back on track when you tend to stray.
> **Marshall Dimock**

goal-orientated. Once you have a conscious target and focus on what you want, you have in effect set a goal, and your subconscious will start working to achieve it.

Your Magical Genie

Your subconscious aims to help you flourish in life, maintain well-being and achieve your every ambition.

Many people are under the illusion that their subconscious is a dark, brooding, or negative place. An analogy that I often find useful in helping people to see their subconscious in a positive light is to suggest they view it as a magical genie. Genies are all-powerful; they can grant wishes and help make your dreams come true. They are loyal, faithful, and obedient. All you need to do to have your every wish or desire granted is to command your genie clearly and precisely by setting a goal. The analogy of the genie also reminds us of one of the most important points to understand about your subconscious; that *it cannot make value judgements.*

Like a fantasy genie, your subconscious cannot distinguish between good or bad, right or wrong, fact or fiction. It doesn't know the difference between what you desire or dread, favour or fear. Just like a genie it can never decide simply to give you something. You must always ask, instruct or command.

> ... the Universe has no choice but to bring you the direct manifestation of your thought about it ... You understand, the creative power is like a genie in a bottle. Your words are its command.
> **NEALE DONALD WALSCH**

> It's not what you are that holds you back, it's what you think you are not.
> **DENIS WAITLEY**

Talking Genie Language

Every thought you think is taken as a command by your subconscious, but it's your strongest thoughts that become true goals.

Your subconscious, like a genie, is commanded by your every

thought, whether pondered internally or verbalized externally. Each of your subconscious thoughts is the equivalent of rubbing your magic lamp. Over time your repeated and strongest thoughts become solidified into beliefs. Each belief that you hold is like a constant command to a magical genie. Your subconscious is goal-orientated, which means that if you are not setting a conscious goal for your subconscious genie to follow, it will simply select your dominant thought, belief, or comment, and pursue that as the goal instead.

Thinking About What You Want

Setting positive, conscious goals is a major challenge for many people. If you were to conduct your own survey and were to ask people: 'What would you like from life?' you would find a startling proportion wouldn't give you a direct answer. Instead, using a process of elimination, they would begin by telling you the opposite, listing all the things they *don't want*: 'I don't want to have more bills than money.' 'I don't want to be unhappy.' 'I don't want to be alone.' 'I don't want to fear the future.'

What few realize is that by thinking repeatedly about what they *don't want*, they are making their *negative thought* the more *dominant*, and thereby a goal for their subconscious to pursue. This sends them into self-sabotage. To achieve what we *do want* we need to learn how to hold our focus on inspiring thoughts and positive desires so our subconscious starts working *with* us rather than against us.

> Habit is either the best of servants or the worst of masters.
> **NATHANIEL EMMONS**
>
> The more you can dream the more you can do.
> **MICHAEL KORDA**

To gain an experience of the great power of consciously commanding your subconscious, please try the following exercise:

Part One

◆ Stand with your feet together. Raise your right arm straight in front of you to shoulder height.

◆ Tilt your head slightly to one side so as to look along the length of your arm.

◆ Now, leaving your arm raised and without moving your feet, see how far you can turn your upper body around to the right.

◆ Go as far as is comfortable, keep looking down your arm, and make a mental note of a point on the wall that indicates how far you have reached.

◆ Return to face the front and lower your arm.

Put the book down and do this first part now!

Part Two

◆ Now repeat the process, but this time use only your mind.

◆ *Do not physically move*. Stay still.

◆ Close your eyes and simply imagine that you are turning. It doesn't matter if you don't see the movement vividly, just think about it or tell yourself you are doing it.

◆ See yourself going round as you did before, only this time tell yourself that it feels so easy that you can go much further.

◆ Tell yourself that you are going at least one metre further than your original point.

◆ Hold your focus for a moment.

◆ Make a mental note that you have passed your original achievement, then return to face the front again and mentally lower your arm.

Put the book down again now, close your eyes for greater impact, and imagine yourself doing part two.

Part Three

◆ Now physically repeat the exercise.

◆ Don't put any more effort into it than you did the first time.

◆ Simply raise your right arm and turn round to the right.

◆ See how much further you go now!

Do the final part now before reading further.

> The future belongs to those who believe in the beauty of their dreams.
> **ELEANOR ROOSEVELT**
>
> Visualize this thing you want. See it, feel it, believe in it. Make your mental blueprint and begin.
> **ROBERT COLLIER**

This exercise is known as Positive Pre-Play and represents the very essence of goal-setting, that is, positively pre-playing or visualizing the outcome you desire before taking physical action.

I use the technique in my own life to rehearse all manner of achievements, and always teach it in my workshops and seminars where virtually everyone discovers that they can go further round the second time. The method works because by thinking or imagining yourself turning further you create a strong command for your subconscious 'genie' to follow. Your subconscious then obeys the command *and works with you* by relaxing and contracting the various muscles that help you achieve your goal.

Top sports people spend an increasing proportion of their training time using visualization techniques such as this to improve their physical performance. By focusing on what you want to achieve, prior to taking physical action, your subconscious helps you to be your best.

The technique works equally well when going for an interview or assessment. I teach it to children in preparation for sitting exams, and use it myself before every presentation as part of the mental preparation.

It isn't necessary to see all of the detail of what you wish to achieve. Simply picture the end result you desire, so as to instruct your subconscious about which strategy to follow. This does not mean that no physical practise is needed. There must be physical experience and practise to produce a thought picture or blueprint command for your subconscious to follow in the first place. However, by choosing your point of focus you enhance the thought pictures of positive outcomes, rather than negative outcomes, and thereby your performance improves.

> You must become the change you wish to see in the world.
> **MAHATMA GANDHI**

> If you want to reach a goal, you must see the reaching in your own mind before you actually arrive at your goal.
> **ZIG ZIGLAR**

The Importance of Repetition, Duration and Emotion

There are three main aspects that make any given thought stronger than another, and thereby a 'dominant command'. They are: *repetition*, *duration* and *emotion*.

The more often you *repeat* the same thought the greater the possibility of it being adopted by your subconscious as a command. A thought that you have accepted as *true* is one that you no longer question, and it therefore becomes a belief. Beliefs are the equivalent of *constant commands* to your subconscious.

The longer the *duration* of time that you hold the belief, the stronger it grows: evolving from a casual opinion to a feeling of certainty and on to a full-blown conviction. As will be discussed in Chapter 2, it's when you begin to attach strong *emotions* to your thoughts and beliefs that you move them onto another level of energy and power altogether. Adding feeling to a thought is like adding a turbo-charger to an engine.

> Great hearts steadily send forth the secret forces that incessantly draw great events.
> **RALPH WALDO EMERSON**

While all thoughts are creative, a thought such as: 'I suppose I'll give it a try' has nowhere near the same level of energy and power as; 'I'm definitely going to do it!' The emotion behind this thought carries a far greater force of belief, determination and certainty. It is obvious which one of the two will stand out most to your subconscious and manifest quickest.

The stronger the emotion, the greater the power of the thought becomes, and the greater the manifestation of that thought.

Thinking a Better Result

My former business partner had been coaching an athlete training for the high jump. The athlete would run, take his jump, and if he jumped well by clearing the bar his habit was to walk back calmly and *unemotionally* to take another practice run. But if he jumped badly and knocked the bar off, he would curse, lose his temper, scream and kick, and became, to say the least, very *emotional*.

Remember, the vast majority of what we do is carried out on autopilot by our subconscious, which always follows the command of our *dominant thought*. Which thought command do you think this athlete was making dominant based on his reactions? By losing his temper he was making the result of his *undesired* performance the dominant command to be selected by his subconscious, because this was the thought to which he attached all his *emotional energy*. The more bothered he became by his occasional mistakes, the more he directed his subconscious towards a result he didn't want, which produced even greater frustration, anger and *emotion*, leading to a rapid downward spiral in his performance.

> Do your work with your whole heart and you will succeed – there's so little competition.
> ELBERT HUBBARD

It's a trap that not only sports people but that all of us slip into in some way or other. The more conscious we become of what we *don't want*, the more we seem to sink into the thought and attract a negative result. To help this man improve his performance my partner encouraged him to do something that we can all use and benefit from in a multitude of different ways in all areas of our lives. Firstly my partner taught him to visualize himself clearing the bar before taking his first step, then to switch his attitude towards his results by helping him to understand that, 'Failure isn't failure if you learn from the experience and have another go.'

When he jumped badly and knocked the bar off, he was instructed to say, calmly and *un-emotionally*: 'I'm learning and improving.' When he jumped really well and cleared the bar, he was encouraged to lift his heart, get excited and celebrate the achievement. This process quickly enhanced his positive thought pattern. He saw himself jumping well, making that the dominant blueprint for his subconscious to follow, and his performance improved greatly.

> One ought to hold on to one's heart; for if one lets it go, one soon loses control of the head too.
> **FRIEDRICH NIETZSCHE**
>
> I am seeking, I am striving, I am in it with all my heart.
> **VINCENT VAN GOGH**
>
> The day will come when, after harnessing space, the winds, the tides and gravitation, we shall harness for God the energies of love. And on that day, for the second time in the history of the world, we shall have discovered fire.
> **TIELHARD DE CHARDIN**

Try visualization and emotional reinforcement yourself next time you are playing any kind of sport, or anything else you want to improve your performance in. This fundamental process is in operation in everything we do, in every area of life.

By adding emotion to a thought we increase its impact on our subconscious and thereby send a powerful command to succeed.

By whatever margin you want to clear the bar, whether by raising your work performance, improving your relationships, or lifting your own self-confidence, you can achieve it by following the same basic goal-setting principle of seeing yourself achieving your desired outcome, with as much energy of the heart as you can possibly muster, before stepping in to physical action.

Why doesn't everyone set Goals?

With so much evidence on the benefits of goal-setting, and with so many great people testifying as to its importance, researchers have long asked the question: 'Why don't more people set goals?'

Traditionally, four main reasons have been identified:

People Don't Realize the Importance of Goals

It is possible to spend years in education, through to higher education, and never once to receive so much as an hour's instruction on the subject of goal-setting. A well-meaning teacher or other person may tell you to set a goal, but this is not true goal-setting and is certainly not the same as receiving information about how your mind works or the principles of success. Unless you are born into a family that sets goals, or come into contact with people who have the habit, the chances are you could go through your entire life without realizing the importance and effectiveness of regular goal-setting.

> High achievement always takes place in the framework of high expectation.
> **JACK AND GARRY KINDER**

People Don't Know How to Set Goals

Some people know that they *should* set goals, but don't know *how* to set them. While goal-setting is a natural mental process, developing it into a powerful tool for achievement is a skill, and like all skills it must be learned. There are right ways and wrong ways, dos and don'ts of goal-setting. Setting a goal wrongly is almost as ineffective as setting no goal at all, because a goal that is not set correctly is unlikely to be achieved. A negative outcome is likely to cause the person to believe that goal-setting doesn't work for them and they may even give up on the idea altogether.

People Fear Rejection

One of man's most basic needs is to be accepted. We learn at an early age that it's not always pleasant to step outside of the norm, or to be too different, and risk being rejected by the majority. Many people hold the distorted belief that if they were to set aspirational goals for themselves and change, that their friends may ridicule them. It's a real fear grounded in fact because some may. However the people whose impulse is to ridicule are rarely real friends, and the usual reason for their negativity is that your goals are a reminder to them that they are not actually doing much with their own life.

If you're anxious about what other people may say about your goals there are two basic ways to overcome the situation. The first is not to tell anyone about your goals, plans or desires, just to keep them to yourself until you have achieved results. The second, and preferable choice is to surround yourself with positive people who will encourage you in all your positive endeavours; this also makes a statement about your belief in yourself. Sharing your goal with a like-minded person is a great step towards its achievement. Every time you tell someone about your goal you are reaffirming the goal to yourself and reinforcing your positive message to your subconscious genie.

Thus to be independent of public opinion is the first formal condition of achieving anything great.
G. W. F. HEGEL

Creative ideas reside in people's minds but are trapped by fear or rejection. Create a judgment-free environment and you'll unleash a torrent of creativity.
ALEX OSBORN

People Fear Failure

Studies conducted around the world have shown that one of the great fears of modern man' is the fear of failure. So strong is this fear in some people that they will avoid failure by not attempting to achieve anything at all. In the workshops I run I have witnessed many people who are excited and inspired by getting in touch with their dream, only to become totally paralyzed by the fear of failure and a lack of self-belief when confronted with committing the goal to paper.

> If you're never scared or embarrassed or hurt, it means you never take any chances.
>
> **JULIA SOREL**

> When you make a mistake, don't look back at it long. Take the reason of the thing into your mind, and then look forward. Mistakes are lessons of wisdom. The past cannot be changed. The future is yet in your power.
>
> **HUGH WHITE**

Some years ago while running a goal-setting session for a large communications company I was encouraging everyone present to set a goal around pursuing their heart's truest desire – to follow their dream. A young man on the programme, who had been quite enthusiastic up until this point, suddenly became very negative and despondent. 'What's the point?' he protested with his arms crossed, 'It's just a dream. It's never going to happen.'

It took me some time, and a fair amount of coaxing, to get him to tell me that his dream was to become a 'Formula One racing car driver'. It took even more time and coaxing to get him to commit the goal onto paper. I never saw him again after that day but about three years later I heard that although he hadn't become a Formula One racing car driver he had got a job with a Formula One team, was now working in the industry he loved, and was earning far more money. He had also become a good amateur rally car driver.

You never know what you can achieve until you try. Reach for the stars and you may only get to the moon, but it is still a great step up. Maybe you'll reach the stars next time.

The fact of the matter is that all success is built on failure. The past and the present do not equal the future. Failure is only failure when no lesson is learnt or you decide to give up without trying again. Failure is always success when it is seen as part of the process of learning. With every attempt that 'goes wrong' valuable feedback is gained. The lessons that are learned today become the foundations for success in the future and just as nature grows, dies and rebuilds, so we sometimes need to fail in order to learn important lessons that become the building blocks of our future achievement. The antidote to the false fear of failure is a success, no matter how small. Achieving a simple goal provides a strong incentive to move on to the next one and the process becomes an upward spiral.

As a final point here please consider that virtually everyone has some fear of stepping outside their comfort zone or exploring new horizons. They, like you, are always setting goals at some level because it's simply the nature of our subconscious mind. The key is to make sure that the goals you are aiming for are what you really want. As Brian Tracy, one of the world's leading experts in setting goals, says: 'Either you learn to set your own goals, or you are destined to spend the rest of your life working for someone who does!

> Never let the shadow of a failure block the sunlight of success.
> **AUTHOR UNKNOWN**
>
> Give a man a fish and feed him for a day, teach a man to fish and let him feed himself for life.
> **AUTHOR UNKNOWN**

Chapter 2

Intention from the Heart

Thoughts that carry the energy of love are turned into powerful wishes that your genie can transform into achievements.

Thinking From the Heart

All emotion empowers intention, and love is the most powerful creative force of all.

Everything splendid, that has ever been created, was created with the power of love. Creating with love, or being heart-centred in your intentions, can range from a simple act of kindness, to feeling passionate about an ongoing project you support, through to dedicating your entire life to a worthy cause. In essence it means that you put your heart into what you do. When you put your heart into your intentions you produce your greatest results, whether that be creating a living, a home, or new life.

A friend of mine once told me about someone he was close to who had died. When the family

> Your vision will become clear only when you look into your heart... Who looks outside, dreams. Who looks inside, awakens.
>
> **CARL JUNG**

gathered after the funeral to share out the person's possessions his sister wanted only one thing: a framed sign that had hung above his fireplace for as long as she could remember. It read, 'Only one life that soon will pass. Only what's done with love will last.'

When we work with the energy of love, work is sweeter, feels easier, and has far reaching consequences that touch the lives of untold numbers of others around us.

Find Your Heart to Find The Flow

Working with heart enables you to find an extra energy – a special magical energy that helps you to flow in whatever you choose to do.

At the time of writing I find myself working harder than ever, for longer hours, with more concentrated effort, and yet the reality is that it has never felt easier, because I love what I do. When you love what you are doing, work flows. When you don't, it grinds.

For some years I have sought to follow my heart and *find the flow* in my life generally, and in all manner of situations specifically, whether digging a ditch, sawing a straight line, writing this book, presenting a seminar, or simply being on the dance floor riding a groove.

The 'flow' is that magical state where everything that you touch feels effortless and falls into place like it's meant to be.

The key to finding flow is to love what you do, and do what you love. You find the flow through holding your intention with heart, not hate. We can all achieve flow in our everyday lives regardless of circumstances because loving what you do is not really about the thing itself –

> If I create from the heart, nearly everything works; if from the head, almost nothing.
> **MARC CHAGALL**

> Neither a lofty degree of intelligence nor imagination nor both together go to the making of genius. Love, love, love, that is the soul of genius.
> **WOLFGANG AMADEUS MOZART**

> The pessimist borrows trouble; the optimist lends encouragement.
>
> **WILLIAM ARTHUR WARD**

> In a full heart there is room for everything, and in an empty heart there is room for nothing.
>
> **ANTONIO PORCHIA**

it's much more about the type of intention you hold and the attitude of mind you project.

Recently, while working to achieve the goal of completing my home extension on time and budget, it became necessary for me to do much of the building work myself, including the backbreaking job of digging the ditches. Because of other work commitments it meant carrying out this task at weekends regardless of the weather. Hence I found myself one cold and rainy Saturday morning, digging a ditch, with water up to my ankles and my clothes soaked through.

The heaviest thing I had swung for some time prior to that day had been a pen across paper, so as I started working at the stony ground with pick and shovel I jarred my body. As the aches and pains began to set into my muscles, negativity crept into my mind like poison. As with most negativity it was self-justifying: 'What on earth am I doing this for? It's not my purpose in life, why don't I just leave it? I could pay somebody else to do it next week. So what if we run over budget and miss the deadline?'

The usual outcome of this type of negative thought pattern is either to talk yourself out of whatever you are doing, or, as I have done so many times in the past, to continue but with a bad heart, begrudging the very act. This always results in the work being painful, the job taking three times as long, the finished result being less then second best, and often needing to be redone. Fortunately, on this particular day, I caught my Low Self being negative, snapped out of the attitude, and chose to play my game of 'finding the flow'. The rules are simple:

◆ Look for reasons to enjoy what you are doing; and

◆ Choose to talk yourself up, by asking, '*What can be great about this?*'

It can be a difficult question to answer, when you are already in a negative mood and your mind is screaming, 'NOTHING!' But the more you ask the question the more you will start to think and feel positive.

The best reason I found for enjoying my work that day was to tell myself, 'What great exercise this is, so much cheaper than going to the gym. It's actually doing me the world of good, and what's more I am getting a free shower at the same time!' This approach may sound a little simplistic but it is actually very profound and has great power. As my mental outlook and self-talk shifted, so my emotional attitude changed. I lightened up, the shovel began to glide, and the workload eased as I found my rhythm and the flow.

> Things turn out best for the people who make the best of the way things turn out.
> **JOHN WOODEN**
>
> The greatest science in the world; in heaven and on earth; is love.
> **MOTHER TERESA**

The same principle holds true in all other situations. You find the flow in what you do by holding your intention with heart, not hate. Projecting positive energy creates momentum. I have found it particularly important to play the 'flow' game whenever I am faced with doing something that I felt unmotivated about, such as getting up really early for a long drive before a presentation, staying away from my family overnight, or working with challenging people. Exercising the power to choose by focusing on what is right about the situation enables you to find extra energy to help you glide through the task. Approach it begrudgingly with negativity and the situation will become worse.

Motivating Emotions

We are not motivated by the logic of our needs. We are motivated by emotion, by the desires of our hearts that stir our blood.

Intention with heart means to create with a positive energy. It means to focus on and feel the positive force of love. Love is the essence of creation. However that does not mean that emotions generally considered to be 'negative' are necessarily bad. Negative emotions have their part to play in creation, and when balanced or naturally channelled, actually produce very positive results. The so-called 'seven deadly sins' are in reality survival instincts that appear across the animal kingdom and are expressed in humans as feelings.

◆ **Envy** stems from an instinct to soak up surrounding resources.

◆ **Pride** is a mating strategy to attract the fittest partner.

◆ **Sloth** is a way of conserving energy and increasing longevity.

◆ **Greed**, in both food and sex, is a way of ensuring that *your* genes are passed on to the next generation.

◆ **Gluttony** is a strategy for preparing for hibernation and surviving the famine between meals.

◆ **Lust** is the guarantee that, no matter how solitary the creature, it will at some stage feel the urge to *mate* and thus perpetuate the species.

◆ Even the explosive energy of **Anger** proves positive by allowing us to call upon great power when bringing down our prey, or escaping those who would prey upon us.

◆ As for **Guilt**: without it we would find it impossible to belong to a family, a pack or group, because we would

> Of all the music that reached farthest into heaven, it is the beating of a loving heart.
> **HENRY WARD BEECHER**

> We know too much and feel too little. At least we feel too little of those creative emotions from which a good life springs.
> **BERTRAND RUSSELL**

commit the most atrocious acts with no sense of remorse.

◆ **Fear** is one of the most beneficial of all emotions as it stops us from putting ourselves into dangerous situations that would otherwise lead to our demise.

Mrs Angry

Look for reasons to be angry, and you'll not only find them, you'll feel them as well.

A few years ago I encountered a very angry woman on one of my workshops who halfway through the programme jumped to her feet and screamed at me: 'I hate my job, but I've got no choice, I've got to do it to pay my bills. How can you stand there telling me that I could feel good about it? You don't know what you're talking about!'

What she had such difficulty in seeing, or hearing, was that her very attitude was perpetuating her trap; and it took me some time to help her to understand that. She might not have enjoyed her work, but it was her dominant thoughts about *hating* it, more than the work itself, that were causing her feelings of bitterness and anger. In turn this made her experience of work even more unpleasant. She was stuck in a thought cycle that was blocking her from moving forwards towards something else.

Gradually, through the workshop she began to understand and accept that being 'OK' about her work was the first step in moving away from it. Acceptance would help her feel differently, which would in turn create a clearer picture of her possible alternatives, and thereby help her find the

> You always do what you want to do. This is true with every act. You may say that you had to do something, or that you were forced to, but actually, whatever you do, you do by choice. Only you have the power to choose for yourself.
>
> W. CLEMENT STONE

motivation to set a goal for what she really did like doing. When you start focusing on what you *do* want, you put your energy into that, thereby moving towards it.

All the time she was telling herself, 'I hate it and there's nothing I can do about it,' she was commanding her subconscious to make her feel bitter, trapped, and helpless. What's more, because she was focused totally on was what she *didn't* want, her subconscious brought her *even more* of it.

All of the aforementioned emotions are *natural* and actually right for us to feel at some time and in some way. However they must be in balance with positive emotions at the other end of the spectrum in order to truly serve us:

◆ **Love** is the prime nurturer of the self and life.

◆ **Compassion** ensures help without self-interest.

◆ **Courage** fosters self-growth and creates security for others.

◆ **Loyalty** strengthens the family, tribe or pack.

◆ **Forgiveness** heals and allows the group to continue.

◆ **Tolerance** makes it possible to live with opposites.

◆ **Peace** is essential for well-being and for all life to flourish.

> The great man is he who does not lose his child's heart.
> **MENCIUS**
>
> No one is truly literate who cannot read his own heart.
> **ERIC HOFFER**

Without these positive balancing qualities, any creature would become isolated and unbalanced, leading to self-destruction.

Animals are governed by instinct, with minimal conscious decision, but as humans we have the power to *choose* our responses and can therefore override our instincts. The gift of choice is a responsible gift and requires us to be aware of ourselves – to know what we are *really* feeling and what the emotion is actually telling us.

Unfortunately for the majority, instead of being clear about their feelings, they often feel confused or emotionally numb. Many people try to avoid uncomfortable emotions altogether and therefore miss their true message and meaning. We are told *implicitly* by society that to feel uncomfortable is bad and wrong in some way. This can often set up a conflict within people experiencing certain negative feelings and lead to cycles of unexpressed emotion, which in turn cause blocks in our development. If left unchecked, these blocks send us spinning out of balance and into some aspect of self-sabotage.

In Chapter 1 I said that everyone has the equivalent of a Low Self and High Self. Your Low Self is made up of your negative animal instincts completely out of balance and in self-sabotage. It projects fear into the future and worries about something that is groundless, or becomes angry at the slightest inconvenience, or uses guilt and anger to control others. In this state our emotions become truly negative and ultimately self-destructive.

The antidote and counterbalance to this downward spiral is to set a positive, heart-centred goal, and thereby activate your High Self: your positive character traits and energies, your best you.

> And now here is my secret, a very simple secret; It is only with the heart that one can see rightly; what is essential is invisible to the eye.
>
> **ANTOINE DE SAINT-EXUPÉRY**

> In every community, there is work to be done. In every nation, there are wounds to heal. In every heart, there is the power to do it.
>
> **MARIANNE WILLIAMSON**

Choosing Your Best You

Through nothing more than *conscious intention* you can choose to generate and project greater amounts of love, patience, and compassion. Love is the greatest creative emotion of all because it is self-generating, self-nourishing and self-sustaining. The more you engage in love, the more love will engage in you, filling your very being with vibrant energy.

Love is in harmony with the natural drive of life and self-evolution or creation. While, in contrast, excessive or misused fear is in alignment with dissolution, destruction, and ultimate self-sabotage.

The universe and all life within it must find its natural balance; likewise we must find our natural balance in order to move forwards in our lives. For instance we are all born with an automatic response system that encourages us to move towards pleasure, and away from pain. The balancing point is dynamic, always changing in accordance with our circumstances and past experience. However, regardless of circumstances the natural emphasis is meant to be towards living in ever-greater pleasure, with only fleeting motivation to move away from the pain or *fear*.

Fear triggers our fight or flight response and can produce great power, but cannot be maintained long term without excessive adrenaline causing damage to our body, mind and emotions. Our negative emotions are there to serve us and act as internal warning signals to avoid dangerous situations, such as the feeling you get when you think you're going to fall. But we were never meant to live our entire lives in continuous fear.

Self-inflicted fear is a by-product of living from our ego, our unbalanced self, and results ultimately in a detrimental outcome. Remember, energy is a creative force, and if you are living in fear, your fear energy will eventually create and attract the very thing that you are trying to escape.

Sadly, I meet many people who spend most of their lives moving away from one type of fear or another. Many of them justify their fear motivation because they believe that it brings results: 'I've got to get it

> You are not here to love the world. You are here to be love in the world.
>
> **GRACE JOHNSTON**

> When I despair, I remember that all through history the way of truth and love has always won. There have been tyrants and murderers and for a time they seem invincible but in the end, they always fall – think of it, ALWAYS.
>
> **MAHATMA GANDHI**

done or I'll be in trouble.' or, 'I've got to earn money to pay my bills.' They argue that this form of motivation is not only logical but spurs them into action. The truth is that pain can be motivating, but not if you start to live your life by it.

Some time ago I worked with a managing director whose father had gone bankrupt when he was a child; the pressure had been a major factor in his parents' subsequent divorce. This had a great impact on my client when he was young and, in an effort to avoid his father's experience, he formed a strong fear-based motivation never to be poor himself.

The negative energy with which he drove himself was also projected outwards onto the people around him. Although he paid reasonable salaries, and professed to love his family, he was a most unpleasant person to be around, and his best people always left his employment.

> There is more hunger for love and appreciation in this world than for bread.
> **MOTHER TERESA**

When I ran my Personal Leadership workshop for his management team he introduced me in this way: 'OK, *everyone, listen up. Brian has come along to talk about being positive and motivated, and I just want to say that you people really need it!'* Then he left the room. In truth, he was the person who most needed the information contained in the workshop, but he had no ear for it. The last I heard he had gone out of business (yet again), and was struggling in his personal relationship. His *unbalanced* fear motivation created his own downfall, and the very result he was trying so hard to avoid.

It can be very hard, even when someone is pointing it out to you, to see and accept when you are justifying a weakness, or self-sabotaging what you love because you are operating from your Low Self.

Those things about us which are most painful to look at, are hardest for us to see.

> It is from numberless diverse acts of courage and belief that human history is shaped. Each time a man stands up for an ideal, or acts to improve the lot of others, or strikes out against injustice, he sends a tiny ripple of hope, and crossing each other from a million different centres of energy and daring those ripples build a current which can sweep down the mightiest walls of oppression and resistance.
>
> **ROBERT F. KENNEDY**

Being able to motivate yourself and inspire others around you is crucial in all forms of businesses or personal endeavour. However, I frequently come into contact with managers and directors who, in a multitude of different ways, are actually extremely de-motivating. Usually these people are well-meaning and have been promoted to their management position because they were very good at their last job, which may have been of a technical nature, but have not been adequately trained or prepared to bring out the best in other people. In the worst cases they start using 'fear motivation', either consciously or unconsciously, in the form of threats and psychological bullying, to get their people engaged in the latest company initiative or scheme.

This negative form of motivation never works long-term. Firstly because it's forced and secondly because it's false: the employees aren't engaged because they want to be, instead they are complying merely out of fear of redundancy. This means that they only ever do *just enough*, and as soon as the fear or threat is removed they revert back to their original position.

In addition, inexperienced managers tend to use the same blanket approach of carrot and stick for everyone. But a positively-motivated person, who knows their own worth, will be extremely *de-motivated* by threats or fear-based incentives, and will choose eventually to move on to a more nurturing environment.

Self-Motivation

*In reality, there is only one true form of motivation,
and that is self-motivation; all else is superficial.*

Each of us at some stage in our development must learn to be
positively self-motivated, because it lies at the very heart of
personal growth. The central teaching in Charles Darwin's
Evolution of Species was not really that the *fittest* survive, but that
those who are the most *adaptable to change* will go on to thrive.

Adaptability to change must be driven from the
inside because it requires a *personal* or individual
response. True self-motivation necessitates that the
individual find their particular balance between pain
and pleasure, and maintains a positive focus on:

◆ *Who* they want to become;

◆ *What* they want to do; and

◆ *Where* they want to go.

Interestingly, a recent scientific study of industry and
commerce showed that *self-awareness* – knowing
yourself and your motivation – was the greatest
indicator of a potential high-flyer, prime for
managerial development.

> **When we direct our thoughts properly, we can control our emotions...**
> **W. CLEMENT STONE**
>
> **The thousand mysteries around us would not trouble but interest us, if only we had cheerful, healthy hearts.**
> **FRIEDRICH NIETZSCHE**

Thinking up Feelings

*We create positive self-motivating emotions by mentally
choosing to operate, or energetically emanate, from our
best qualities, our High Self.*

Thoughts create feelings. Each of your thoughts carries or triggers
another energy: emotion. Try it for yourself:

Sit down and think of something sad that has

happened to you either recently or in the distant past. You'll find that within a few moments you start to feel sad.

Likewise if you choose to focus on something positive, within a few moments the thought will trigger the release of feelings: this time positive nourishing ones that make you feel happy.
Thinking positive thoughts is motivating, which in turn influences your actions and causes positive effects in your life.

When I first encountered the concept of personal development, although I quickly understood the importance of focusing on positive thoughts, it was something that I found quite difficult to do. Being consistently heart-centred didn't come easily to me. I had gone through the experience of losing so much that I held dear, and had become so insecure in myself, that I feared being too optimistic in case I became overwhelmed again by disappointment. In the process I had become a little bitter and negative. The outlook that I started to hold was that being *soft* in any way was a weakness that would lead only to greater misfortune.

Fortunately the practise of personal development raised my self-awareness and helped me to see beyond this false fear. It was the very struggle of trying to hold a positive outlook that led me to explore goal-setting and eventually to the discovery of the Goal Mapping technique.

I have used Goal Mapping consistently to move beyond my fear and on to new horizons. Through the journey I have learnt that qualities such as *courage* and *strength* don't come from being hard; they develop from showing *care*, *compassion*, and *love*. As Benjamin Hoff puts it so brilliantly in his excellent book *The Tao of Pooh*: 'With care comes courage and also wisdom... those who have no compassion have no wisdom. Knowledge, yes; cleverness, maybe;

> We must walk consciously only part way toward our goal and then leap in the dark to our success
> HENRY DAVID THOREAU

wisdom, no. A clever mind is not a heart. Knowledge doesn't care. Wisdom does.'

The more I learnt that being *heart-centred* isn't weak, it's strong, the more I found the courage to open my heart and my development became an upward spiral. Gradually, as I held onto the central goal of enlivening my High Self by focusing on being my best, I was able to dissipate my various fears, and find the courage to follow the vision of my heart.

> A difficult time can be more readily endured if we retain the conviction that our existence holds a purpose – a cause to pursue, a person to love, a goal to achieve.
> **JOHN MAXWELL**

Ancient Pictures and Modern Words

Do you hear what I'm saying, or see what I mean?

We all think in pictures. It is the way that a young child learns initially to comprehend things, and was the way that we thought originally as a species. Just think of the way a young child responds to a picture of an apple on a flash card and recognizes that it represents the fruit, long before understanding the letters beneath the picture that relate to the same item. Thinking in words is something that we have learnt comparatively recently in our development as a species, and likewise it happens relatively late in our early development as children. First we begin to understand spoken language and then we begin hearing it as thoughts talking in our head.

From birth through to about the age of five, both sides of our brain – the logical left-brain and the emotional right-brain – are naturally in balance. Gradually, as we learn to speak, and more particularly when we learn to read and write, we become more left-brain dominant, and thereby much more aware of our verbal thought process – the internal chatter inside our heads – than we are of the fleeting right-brain pictures that flash through our mind.

It's almost like having two different brains inside your head; like two cogs running at different speeds.

> There can be no knowledge without emotion. We may be aware of a truth, yet until we have felt its force, it is not ours. To the cognition of the brain must be added the experience of the soul.
> **ARNOLD BENNETT**

> There is one quality that one must possess to win, and that is definiteness of purpose, the knowledge of what one wants, and a burning desire to possess it.
>
> **NAPOLEON HILL**

It's only when you slow down, perhaps by relaxing in a hot bath, or just before you are about to go to sleep, that the cogs synchronize and you suddenly have a great idea or flash of insight.

The reason we have two sides to our brain is because we *need* two sides to our brain. When balanced they help us to be at our very best. With our right-brain, which possesses the quality of imagination, we are able to look forward, visualize our future, and sense how it might feel. With our left-brain, which is gifted with logic, we are able to identify the best path and strategy to achieve our vision and the major steps leading towards it.

To achieve a positive mental balance you must *lead from the right* and *manage from the left*.

Always lead from your emotional right-brain. Not only is it the forward-looking side of your brain, it is also the side that is connected to your heart. While in contrast, your left-brain, which looks backward through memory, processes thought through logic and is connected to your ego and fear.

Goal Mapping

Combining right-brain pictures with left-brain words.

The Goal Mapping technique captures this natural combination of pictures and words and through it provides great power for whoever uses it. Look around the world at all forms of ancient communication and you will quickly discover that they are based on pictures or images. Egyptian hieroglyphics, North American sand paintings, Asian rice paintings, Aboriginal rock paintings, and eastern prayer flag mandalas, not only represent the ways people communicated with each other, but also the way that people, for thousands of years, set their intentions.

Even after the advent of structured language and the written word people still continued to set their intentions using symbols and imagery. Only in the last seventy years or so with the rise of psychoanalytic and management techniques have written goal statements become the norm in the western world.

However, the core effectiveness of any type of goal-setting technique lies in the ability of the technique to communicate conscious intentions and motivating emotions in a way sufficiently powerful that they become the dominant command to your subconscious.

In recent years the use of powerful brain-scanning equipment has been able to prove what the ancients always knew: that the major path to the subconscious is through the right-brain and pictures. The left-brain and words have a much weaker connection which is why a goal that is communicated only in words must be re-written hundreds of times to achieve the same power as one created through pictures or symbols. As the saying goes: a picture is worth a thousand words.

Goal Mapping is a communication link to your subconscious 'genie'. It is a way of conveying your intentions with heart, in words and pictures, emotion and logic, so that your subconscious understands clearly what you choose to achieve, and helps you move forward in life.

Chapter 3

Climbing the LIFT Ladder

The path that leads to your goals will feature many obstacles: there will be ruts to scrabble out of, hurdles to climb over, and chasms to clear. Following the seven principles of LIFT is like having a ladder to serve you on your journey.

The Seven Principles of LIFT

LIFT stands for *Life, Information, For, Transcendence* and is the name of the company that I founded with my wife Sangeeta to help people evolve to higher levels of success. The seven principles of LIFT are actually seven strategies for personal empowerment or suggested ways of being. They represent the basis of our teaching for success in life and conscious self-evolution. Collectively the principles act as the foundations for the Goal Mapping technique and provide a complete approach to life. Each principle builds on the last, like rungs on a ladder that enable the user to overcome challenges and move to higher levels of awareness and effectiveness.

Each of the seven principles is fundamental to the process of conscious success. They are multidimensional and universal principles that are applicable individually or collectively to a single situation and point in time, through to a life-plan spanning many years. Together the principles of LIFT form a cohesive programme for achieving successful outcomes, steering self-growth, and a philosophy for evaluating important life choices.

Principle 1 – Raise Your Awareness

Whatever decision you need to make, whatever challenge you want to overcome, whatever goal you wish to achieve, raising your awareness will be the first step towards it.

Raising awareness of yourself and your current situation, and recognizing the likely outcomes of your intended actions, or continued inaction, are always the first steps towards clearing the fog of personal confusion, overcoming procrastination, and developing self-motivation.

Although you want to change your current situation, your current level of awareness will not be sufficient to take you to the next level of your growth, the next stage in your journey or the next goal on your life path or purpose; that will require a new and higher level of awareness.

Our effectiveness in life is linked very closely to our conscious general awareness and awareness of ourselves. The more aware we become of our own habits, desires and motivations, the more effective we can be in choosing regularly to be at our best, thereby producing our best results. The more aware we are of other people, their habits and desires, strengths and weaknesses, the more successful we can

> Knowledge is power.
> **FRANCIS BACON**
>
> Be ye transformed by the renewal of your mind, that ye may prove what is good and acceptable and perfect, the will of God.
> **ROMANS 12.2**

be in creating harmony and synergy. The more aware we are of our environment, whether a city or jungle, the more able we are to live in harmony with it, adapting aspects of it to meet our particular requirements, while maintaining its own natural balance

Personal Picture Paradigms

We all create internal thought pictures of understanding and then project them onto the world about us.

Our overall awareness of our self, a situation, or the world in general, is known as a *paradigm*. A paradigm is a general viewpoint that is held about something or someone, and acts as a guidance grid for our opinions, attitudes, and actions.

Each paradigm that we hold is a personal view that we project out onto the world and everything in it. It is the *map* or blueprint that our subconscious reads constantly to regulate our actions and re-actions.

When you woke up this morning you probably didn't need to think through *who* you are or *how* you deal with the world, because you have built up *paradigm pictures* of how you act and react to the various situations in your life. It's these paradigm pictures that inform your subconscious about how you behave in any given situation, without the need for constant rational thought. Likewise it is your paradigm pictures that allow you to drive your car, ride your bike, walk, and all manner of other routine activities that we take for granted, all achieved without conscious effort.

The disadvantage of personal paradigms is that once you have created them, they become *set* or fixed as if written in stone, while in reality everything around us is fluid, flexible, and constantly changing.

> How little do we know of that which we are! How less that we may be!
> **BYRON**

> Each man's belief is right in his own eyes.
> **WILLIAM COWPER**

> There is nothing either good or bad, but thinking makes it so.
> **WILLIAM SHAKESPEARE**

Looking at the Future from the Past

Over the years I have come to trust my intuition and was pleasantly surprised when I started working with top executives to find that they did likewise. After running their left-brain critical analyses, they will still make a final decision based on gut feeling.

Some years ago I received an unexpected phone call from an old client company asking me if I was available to do some training for them at short notice. I found myself saying *yes* very happily without any real thought or questioning. It was only after I had put the phone down that I got a gut feeling – right-brain intuition – that something wasn't quite right.

It was when I started listening to my right-brain feelings that I realized I had said 'yes' to this organization based on a paradigm of the past, without checking that my knowledge matched the realities of the present. I began to raise my awareness by questioning my client further and learnt that the nature of the work they wanted me to do was significantly different to that undertaken previously and was not in alignment with my core teaching. In a heartbeat my paradigm, together with my opinion of the opportunity, changed completely and I declined their offer.

The same happens in other areas of our lives. We often judge a situation in a certain way, and then something happens that causes us to see the situation in another way entirely, then our view – our paradigm – shifts completely.

> There is a road from the eye to heart that does not go through the intellect.
> **G. K. CHESTERTON**
>
> The first rule is to keep an untroubled spirit. The second is to look things in the face and know them for what they are.
> **MARCUS AURELIUS**

Our paradigms determine our opinions, attitudes and behaviours and therefore the results we create. If we are to respond correctly to the multitude of situations and choices that come our way, and steer towards the achievement of our goals, then we must learn to gain *clarity on reality* by choosing to raise our awareness, through conscious thought and questions.

A distorted paradigm, leads to distorted opinions, attitudes and actions, which in turn create distorted results.

Principle 2 – Develop Possibility Consciousness

The past and the present do not equal the future. The future exists in infinite possibilities. By developing an open-minded approach, we capture our highest opportunity.

Whenever I find myself stuck or unsure in any area of my life I climb the first rung of the LIFT ladder by asking myself the question: 'Have I raised my awareness sufficiently in this situation?' I then climb the second rung to remind myself to *develop possibility consciousness*, that is, have an open mind.

In order to raise your awareness you need to keep an open mind and consider all possibilities. Too often people approach a situation with their views influenced by an experience from the past. But the past and the present do not equal the future. The future is unwritten, evolving, and always in some way different from before.

> A mind that is stretched to a new idea never returns to its original dimension.
> **OLIVER WENDELL HOLMES**

> Our task now is not to fix blame for the past, but to fix the course for the future.
> **JOHN F. KENNEDY**

Do You See It?

In the 1950s a pioneer named William Beebe led the world in deep-sea exploration. He was the first person to descend to great depths in a bathysphere. The creatures he described were so far beyond the paradigms of the established scientists of the time that his observations were dismissed as fanciful. Only now, with the use of advanced submersibles, are his claims being verified. But even today the life recorded at these great depths is so fantastic and beyond the common paradigm that we often lack adequate language to describe the texture, movement, and colours of deep-sea species.

Throughout history those who have claimed to be aware of a level of reality that others do not perceive have been ridiculed, discredited, and sometimes crucified for speaking their truths.

Selective Perception

We don't really see the reality of life as it truly is – we see life through our interpretation of reality – we see life as we are.

It is estimated that the body, via the senses, receives around 2,000,000 pieces of information or *stimuli* from the world around us every single moment of the day. However, our conscious thinking mind can process or *hold* only about nine digits of information at any one time. An area of our brain called the Reticular Activating System (RAS) acts as a filter to screen out information it deems irrelevant and passes on only that which is considered important. It protects our conscious mind from being over-whelmed by data.

> Man is not what he thinks he is, but what he thinks, he is!
> RALPH WALDO EMERSON

> For the person who is good with the hammer, everything in life tends to look like a nail.
> ABRAHAM MASLOW

While this automatic process is meant to serve us, it can sometimes be severely limiting. If you do not select the paradigm filter for your RAS by choosing consciously to have an open mind, it will set itself auto-matically in alignment with your dominant thoughts and opinions or beliefs.

It is this process that leads to the common experience of, having bought a new car, starting to notice similar cars everywhere you go. The cars were always there, but getting one yourself created a new dominant thought that programmed your RAS to pass on all information concerning that subject. The same thing happens if you are expecting a baby: you start seeing babies everywhere; if you book a holiday you will see constant reminders of your destination.

Because your RAS is part of your subconscious, and your subconscious does not make value judgements about right or wrong, a negative limiting thought, such as '*I can't*' will become a filter for your RAS, leading you to block out valuable information to the contrary, such as '*I can*'.

Spotting Opportunities

Some years ago a friend of mind was made redundant from a job that he loved dearly. The experience hit him hard and he sunk into depression, becoming quite bitter. Anyone who asked him how he was doing got the same basic reply: '*Destined for the scrap heap, that's how I am. No opportunities for me out there now – not at my age. I'm going to spend the rest of my life on welfare.*'

> We don't see things as they are, we see them as we are.
> **ANAÏS NIN**
>
> Every man takes the limits of his vision, for the limits of the world.
> **ARTHUR SCHOPENHAUER**

He said this to virtually everyone he met but the person who heard it *most* was himself. It soon became a dominant thought filter for his RAS. I lost count of how many times when I was with him, I would spot an opportunity for decent paid work and an income; whenever I mentioned it to him he would reply: '*I didn't hear that,*' or '*I didn't see that*'. He had been in the same place as me, had spoken to the same people as me, and was surrounded by the same information as me. Even though his ears and eyes picked up on the opportunity, he had programmed himself to see only lack, limitation and difficulty, and so that was all his RAS passed on to his conscious awareness.

When you set a goal, you are not just stating your intentions, you are setting a command for your Reticular Activating System, which then helps you to see beyond any preconceived limitations, and spot new visions of opportunity, potential and abundance.

Principle 3 – Find Balance

In all the world, there can be no lasting success without balance.

We live on a planet that spins in a balanced orbit, with balanced climates, that support balanced eco-systems, where a multitude of species live in balanced co-existence, and within which each individual creature must maintain balance in its physical body and surroundings to survive. In short, success is balance, and balance is success.

In the Goal Mapping workshops I run, when I ask people, 'What would you most like to achieve in your Goal Mapping session?' The most common answer is: 'Greater balance between my home life and work life.' I have heard similar things in my sessions with children, who want more balance between study and play.

Balance makes life work well. You will always know when you are in balance because you will feel really good about yourself inwardly, and this will reflect in your life outwardly. Likewise you will also know when you or your life is out of balance, because everything will start falling apart.

Everyone's balancing point will be slightly different and unique to them. What one person may need to do more of to achieve balance, another may actually need to do less of. However, as a general guide I recommend that you consider six key areas to achieve balance within and between.

Try this exercise:

> Give your self a score of between 1–10 in each of the following areas. Measure only your own life balance, do not compare yourself with anyone else, that way the exercise is always relevant. Be intuitive and listen for the first number that comes to mind.

> Even a happy life cannot be without a measure of darkness, and the word happiness would lose its meaning if it were not balanced by sadness.
>
> **CARL JUNG**

Mental ....   Emotional ....   Physical ....
Financial ....   Social ....   Spiritual ....

Next plot your scores onto the wheel below, starting from the top spoke (Mental) and moving round the wheel clockwise placing a score on each spoke.

What is right for one soul may not be right for another. It may mean having to stand on your own and do something strange in the eyes of others. But do not be daunted. Do whatever it is because you know within it is right for you.

EILEEN CADDY

Blessed are the flexible, for they shall not be bent out of shape.

AUTHOR UNKNOWN

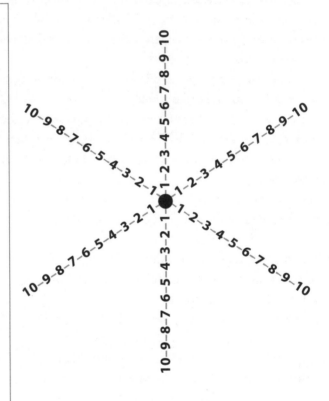

The life-balance wheel

Finally, link the numbers you have ringed by going around the outside, like a dot-to-dot puzzle. This will give you a 'life-wheel': a picture of your current sense of balance.

The ideal is to have high scores in each area combined with an even circle or wheel. Most people tend to have a flat area or dip at some point. If this is true for you, please see it as a positive result; it indicates where you need to put your focus and energy in order to bring your self and life into a greater level of balance and success.

By focusing on the flat point in your wheel, and setting yourself a goal to improve it, you in effect *lift* all the other areas automatically. For instance some time ago after going through the exercise for myself I saw that my flat area was the physical spoke. I had stopped taking exercise, my diet had been poor, and as a result my health had suffered. I set a goal to get up half an hour earlier three times a week in order to take exercise. Within a short period I had improved my physical well-being, and the new level of balance was positively affecting all the other areas of my life. I was sharper *mentally*, I felt happier *emotionally*, I had more energy, which made a difference *financially*. *Socially* I was a much nicer person to be around, and *spiritually* I felt more connected. Through bringing my self and my life back into balance I had produced a 'synergy of self'.

> I don't want to get to the end of my life and find that I have just lived the length of it. I want to have lived the width of it as well.
>
> **DIANE ACKERMAN**

> We cannot be happy if we expect to live all the time at the highest peak of intensity. Happiness is not a matter of intensity, but of balance and order and rhythm and harmony.
>
> **THOMAS MERTON**

Synergy of Self

The fruits of balance.

By achieving balance across all major life areas you achieve 'synergy of self'. *Synergy*, meaning that together the whole is greater than the sum of its parts, is a naturally occurring dynamic. Synergy is not created through sameness, it is created through complementary or *balanced* difference. Eco-systems when balanced become synergistic. Interdependent species are synergistic. People, when they are balanced enough to respect the differences between each other, are synergistic. Likewise each of us, when we are balanced in ourselves, produces 'synergy of self' and a shift to a higher level of awareness, well-being, effectiveness and success.

While we each have many balancing points, one of the most important, because it is fundamental and impacts on all other areas, is finding the mental balance between our left- and right-brain thinking.

Whole-Brain Balance

Choose your destination through your right-brain, but use your left-brain to organize the journey.

Although there is still much scientific debate about the nature of true genius, it is apparent that some of the greatest people throughout history were equally brilliant with both sides of their brain. For instance Leonardo da Vinci, credited by many as the most brilliant mind ever known, was not only a great artist but also a great scientist; even his working notes are a mixture of words and pictures on the same page. Likewise Mozart, although known for his superb music, could have applied his mind easily to becoming one of the world's leading mathematicians. Great people tend to have great balance in their thinking.

> **If we insist on looking at the rainbow of intelligence through a single filter, many minds will erroneously seem devoid of light.**
> **RENÉE FULLER**

Everyone enters the world with the brain balanced naturally and they stay that way for about the first five years of life. Scientists estimate that our ability to learn in this period of balanced brain activity is about 20–25 times greater than it is in adults. Unfortunately the majority of people become *unbalanced* in their brain function as they grow older. Typically, in the western world, we are left-brain dominant. This may have arisen via a myriad of causes such as genetic influence, childhood conditioning, schooling, choice of profession, and society in general. However, regaining whole-brain balance can be achieved by anyone, simply by setting a goal to do so. It is the very act of having a goal and creating a Goal Map that helps you to gain greater balance.

The brain is like a muscle; if we stop using any aspect of it, it begins to waste, but never completely dies. Doing thinking exercises, just like working muscles at the gym, can enliven our brain, and re-gain brain balance, moving the self onto another level of effectiveness. In addition, the seven steps of the Goal Mapping technique are designed to exercise both sides of your brain and help you create whole-brain balance, while your goal itself helps you maintain balance in your life.

Dynamic Balance

A movement with repose.

The right-brain gazes forwards with the quality of imagination, while the left-brain analyzes backwards through memory. Our right-brain is emotional, our left-brain logical. Our right-brain leans towards being passive, while our left-brain is active. Finding the balance between the two halves of the brain does not mean finding a static balancing point such as on a set of scales. Brain balance, like other natural checks and balances, is a dynamic process. It is *iterative*, interactive, shifting the point of focus and balance constantly from one side to the other, like a flowing figure eight on its side.

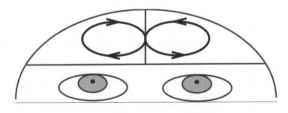

Brain balance

> In the power to change yourself is the power to change the world around you.
> **ANWAR SADAT**

> Our greatest battles are those with our own minds.
> **JAMESON FRANK**

> Neutral is a state where you are not jumping ahead too quickly or moving too slow. Neutral does not mean being inactive, complacent or passive. It's about a calm poise that allows for new information and new possibilities to emerge before taking further action. When in neutral you actually increase your sensitivity and intuitive intelligence. Neutral is fertile ground for new possibilities to grow from.
> **DOC CHILDRE**

> What's going on in the inside shows on the outside.
> **EARL NIGHTINGALE**

As you begin to find your balance inside your head through choosing your focus, so you will start to reap the benefits on the outside, by generating greater flow and harmony in your life.

This is something that I have been practising for many years, by exercising my right-brain through visualizing; my left-brain through strategizing; and anchoring the balance through the Goal Mapping technique. In addition, whenever I need to evaluate a situation or opportunity I use the LIFT ladder, and after climbing the first two rungs (see above) I move onto the third rung by asking myself: 'If I take this opportunity, follow this direction, or pursue this goal, will it help me achieve more, or less, *balance* in my life?

Principle 4 – Be on Purpose

Purpose is to a person what fuel is to an engine – without it we end up going nowhere.

> It is strange that though all must tread the path of life, so few know whither they are going.
> **DR PIERRE SCHMIDT**
>
> Let us follow our destiny, ebb and flow. Whatever may happen, we master fortune by accepting it.
> **VIRGIL**

Everyone is born with a purpose, a reason for being, something they can excel at. When you are '*on purpose*' you find your passion, your power, your flow, and it feels as if life is working with you. When you are not on purpose, you are off-track; your power to create is dissipated and every last chore seems to drag.

To be on purpose, you must first find or *know* your purpose; you must discover 'that thing that makes your heart sing': the thing that you are passionate about. This is one of the great inherent goals that each of us is born with. Everyone has a purpose and pursuing it is a life goal.

Somewhere between the first and third centuries BC, Patanjali wrote:

'When you are inspired by some great purpose, some
 extraordinary project, all your thoughts break their
 bonds;
Your mind transcends limitations, your consciousness
 expands in every direction, and you find yourself in a
 new, great and wonderful world.
Dormant forces, faculties and talents become alive, and
 you discover [yourself] to be a greater person by far
 than you ever dreamed yourself to be.'

Seeking the True Fuel

*Motivation comes from inspiration, which is powered by
purpose.*

I began my career as a speaker and trainer with a personal development company based in London, making one-hour presentations on self-improvement. I was usually introduced at my speaking engagements as a motivational speaker, but something about that title never felt completely right for me. Even though my presentations were generally well received, I quickly realized that to call the content motivational wasn't really the truth.

I was popular, probably because I was entertaining, but the focus of the presentation was not so much motivation as hype, using the combined approach of carrot and stick, pain and pleasure. I was using the same approach in my own life. If I needed to do something that I didn't feel motivated about I would either tell myself how much pain I would be in if I didn't do it or I would focus on how much pleasure I would feel once my goal was achieved.

> A man is a success if he gets up in the morning and goes to bed at night and in between does what he wants to do.
> **BOB DYLAN**

There's no doubt that these strategies work; people have used them on themselves and others for countless generations. The challenge is their application as a continuous process, putting yourself or others under the threat of pain, or in the hope of pleasure constantly, in order to create momentum.

In contrast, I noticed that people I admired didn't need to do that. They seemed to have more naturally balanced motivation; as I studied them further I saw where their motivation came from: *inspiration*. Inspired people do not need to consciously motivate themselves, it is a natural product of their inspiration. They have a different spring in their step. They are 'naturally motivated'. So my question then became: 'Where does inspiration rise from?'

> Great minds have purposes, others have wishes.
> **WASHINGTON IRVING**
>
> A person without a definite purpose in life is more handicapped than the most disadvantaged or disabled.
> **LESLIE FIEGER**

While I knew that momentary inspiration springs from our divinity, and that people in every generation have inspired others, I also knew that this type of inspiration is like receiving a spark that lights the fire: in order for it to become a burning passion, the individual themselves must feed the flames. The fuel that keeps the fire of life burning is having a sense of meaning and purpose; that is the true root of inspiration that feeds motivation.

A Sense of Purpose

Find that thing that makes your heart sing, and then find a way to make your living your life.

Purpose and goals are different. A goal is tangible, quantifiable. It has a definite achievement date. A purpose, on the other hand, is an ongoing endeavour, a long-term mission, or life vision. Purpose is the direction; goals are the significant milestones along the way.

There are many different types of purpose. For some people purpose will be the achievement of something physical: winning, buying, building, or *having*. For other people, purpose will be centred on their work, project, career, or what they are *doing*.

Your prime purpose is always *to be your best*. This is the purpose that all life is born with. By seeking to *be* your best person, you naturally *do* your best work, and invariably *have* your best results. *Be-Do-Have* is the *syntax* or sequence for success.

Always *be* first as it produces the right attitudes that empower what we *do*, which in turn enhances the results we *have*. In addition, as humans we have the free will to influence our natural urge to become the best we can be, and to use it as the force to carry us forward towards our heartfelt desires and dreams.

Whichever level or type of purpose you choose to pursue, it will mean climbing the LIFT ladder in some way by:

◆ Raising your awareness;

◆ Developing possibility consciousness; and

◆ Finding balance.

On reaching the fourth rung of the LIFT ladder, ask yourself the question: 'If I take this opportunity or direction, will it move me closer towards the achievement of my purpose, or will it take me subtly off track?' The question is key. I am often offered opportunities that look on the surface to be attractive, but on closer examination they are not in alignment with my chosen purpose and direction. It is actually much easier to say *no* to something that is not right for you when you're really clear about your big *yes* – your purpose.

There are a number of ways to find your purpose. Sometimes it will reveal itself quickly, sometimes it will unfold over many years; but always it will begin with setting a goal to 'know' what it is.

> You can't wait for inspiration. You have to go after it with a club.
> **JACK LONDON**

> The least of things with a meaning is worth more in life than the greatest of things without it.
> **CARL GUSTAV JUNG**

Principle 5 – Become Fully Response-Able

Responsibility equals 'the ability to choose your response'. It is the key to your greatest freedom and ultimate success.

> A man who is master of himself can end a sorrow as easily as he can invent a pleasure.
>
> **OSCAR WILDE**
>
> If you are distressed by anything external, the pain is not due to the thing itself but to your own estimate of it; and this you have the power to revoke.
>
> **MARCUS AURELIUS**

Growing up without the ability to read or write properly I often guessed at the meaning of words depending on how they were used in a sentence. The context in which I usually heard the word responsibility was: 'Brian, are you going to *take responsibility* for this?', which always sounded to me like taking *blame*; so that's what I came to believe responsibility meant.

When I learnt to read well and started educating myself I looked up the true meaning of responsibility; it means 'the ability to *choose* your response'. It had never dawned on me before that responsibility was *response-ability*: the power to choose. Because I associated it with blame I had tried my best to avoid it whenever possible; now I saw it for its true power and started to positively embrace it. The paradigm shift changed my life completely, and the more I practised response-ability, the more empowered I became.

The opposite of response-ability is blame, and during my early years I had developed the habit of blaming everyone and everything for any aspect of myself or my life that I didn't like. I blamed the government for the recession and collapse of my business; I blamed the banks for stopping their funding and for me losing my home; and I blamed my wife for causing the breakdown of our marriage.

The real trouble with blame is that it's always *'out there'* – outside of yourself and always somebody else's fault – which means you have little influence over it. This results in you feeling as if someone is doing something *to* you, or *making* you feel a certain way, and that you are powerless to do anything about it. Blame turns you in to a victim.

Once I raised my self-awareness and focused on the fundamental success principles of life, I started exercising response-ability. The first step was to drop all those old excuses and replace them with consciously-chosen, goal-led affirmations: I am patient, I am tolerant, I am response-able.

The hardest part was accepting that I had made mistakes, got my perspective wrong and had messed things up, but that it was *all right* so long as I learnt from the experiences. Once I shifted my perspective and stopped seeing responsibility as blame and fault, I started taking ownership of my challenges. There is great power in this. If there is something you don't like in your life but you acknowledge you had a hand in creating it, naturally it means that you are empowered to *change it* and create something else if you please. If, on the other hand, you persist in blaming something or someone else rather than looking at your self then you will always feel trapped and act like a victim.

Every so often I meet someone who believes, as I used to, that you are the way you are, and there's nothing you can do about it. Some even argue for their weaknesses, rolling out the same old reasons why they can't change: it's their genes, their parents, or their environment that's making them the way they are; but these are only *influences* not determinants. While we may sometimes be limited in our physical options we are always totally free to choose our mental and emotional response. We can choose to be our best.

It is learning to choose a positive response to

> There are two big forces at work, external and internal. We have very little control over external forces such as tornados, earthquakes, floods, disasters, illness and pain. What really matters is internal force. How do I respond to those disasters? Over that I have complete control.
>
> **LEO BUSCAGLIA**

> ... being judgmental about your own behavior is actually another cop-out because it makes you feel as though you're doing something virtuous.
>
> **BARBARA SHER**

> The ancestor of every action is a thought.
>
> **RALPH WALDO EMERSON**

negative situations that allows us ultimately to triumph. Hence the ancient truth: 'It's not what happens in life that makes the biggest difference, it's how you respond to what happens.' Response-ability is the birthplace of inner freedom and the foundation of personal power. Practise choosing your response to the little things, and as you strengthen your power, it will become easier to choose your response to the big things.

When I measure myself now against where I've come from I realize just how far I've travelled and how much I've grown. Even though there are still aspects of myself that I want to improve, I know that if I hadn't discovered the magic of response-ability and goal-setting I would never have embarked on the journey in the first place.

Self-actualization

Change the way that you think about everything and everything about you will change.

Thought stimulates creation. Everything that has ever been created in the history of the world began as someone's idea. Every great work of art, every empire, every achievement, was once just a thought in somebody's head. Likewise every habit, every action, and every emotion also begins as a thought.

Thought creates emotion, and the combination of thought plus emotion begins to influence our behaviour. Repeated behaviour becomes habit. Habits shape our circumstances, which in turn trigger more thoughts of either acceptance or rejection of our circumstances, and the cycle continues again.

We all live in a self-actualization cycle like the one above right. The cycle can either lift us up towards personal development, or send us spiralling

> As human beings, our greatness lies not so much in being able to remake the world – that is the myth of the atomic age – as in being able to remake ourselves.
> **Mahatma Gandhi**

> Every dawn, each man is offered, again, the freedom of choice...
> While life remains, there is always the opportunity to remake the world.
> **Jim Coleman**

> Between stimulus and response, there is a space. In that space lies our freedom and power to choose our response. In our response lies our growth and freedom.
> **Victor Frankl**

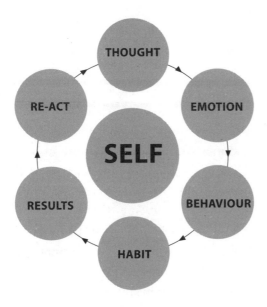

Self-actualization cycle

down into personal decline. The choice is invariably ours regardless of circumstances, because the cycle always begins with a thought, and *that* we are totally free to choose.

The key with this principle and rung of the *LIFT* ladder is to ask your self: 'Am I consciously and proactively choosing my response, or am I being reactive, unconscious, and giving away my power?'

Principle 6 – Maintain a Positive Focus

Think about what you want, not what you fear.

We live in a constant state of becoming – continually changing, perpetually self-manifesting. It is as if the universe responds to our energy and manifests or creates in accordance with our wishes. Our ability to wish and control what the universe creates for us lies in our ability to choose our focus. It is our 'response-ability' because nobody else can do it for us. Each individual must choose the direction of their focus, which in turn steers the direction of life and the quality of what we create and attract through the universe.

When you choose to focus on the positive in your life, your self, your situations, you generate an energy that, like radio waves, transmits your intention and attracts back the people, things and situations that are in harmony with it. The same thing happens when you focus on the negative, only this time you set up a negative attraction.

By taking response-ability for the focus of your thoughts and choosing to concentrate on the positive, you cause an effect in all the areas your cycle of self-actualization and create a positive chain reaction. Your mind becomes inspired; your emotions become motivating, your behaviour has purpose; your habits are empowering; and you design your life consciously. Any justification or blame turns into feedback and learning.

At each stage of the cycle the power grows stronger and the attraction or creation energy becomes greater. Anyone who has ever worked to end an addiction like smoking will know that it's much easier to break the cycle at the mental level of thought, than it is once it reaches the physical level of habit and craving.

With all forms of creation, whether of a new habit, or the achievement of an external goal, the key is to 'maintain a positive focus' and in so doing you'll raise your awareness, increase your energy and begin to operate from your *super-conscious mind*.

> The mind is its own place, And in itself, can make a Heav'n of Hell, or a Hell of Heav'n.
> **JOHN MILTON**

> I learnt that nothing is impossible when we follow our inner guidance, even when its direction may threaten us by reversing our usual logic.
> **GERALD JAMPOLSKY**

Your Super-conscious Mind

Intuition on tap, just ask.

Your super-conscious is that part of your mind that is connected to your High Self and collective or universal consciousness. Thought is energy and energy never dies, it simply changes vibration and form. Each person's individual consciousness is like a wave rising up from the ocean. At the end of its individual existence it doesn't actually cease, it simply merges back with the whole again.

By maintaining a positive focus, you attain a state of mind where your super-conscious begins to bring you insights and ideas from the ocean of collective consciousness: thoughts that you hadn't already conceived or considered in any way. Many great people have testified to the power of the super-conscious and have credited it with their highest achievements.

Thomas Edison, the greatest inventor of the twentieth century, declared that he never had an original idea, instead he simply plucked them from the air. Mozart stated that many of his compositions came to him *fully formed*, complete in every detail, but he was hearing them in his mind for the very first time.

This mental faculty isn't the reserve only of great historic figures; they learnt to use what is available to all of us. While it's your subconscious mind that deals with pattern recognition, such as spotting lots of cars like yours, it's your super-conscious mind that deals with *precognition* and inspiration. Many people have experienced receiving insights prior to an event. In its milder form precognition is a hunch; when full blown it's a complete vision of what to do, where to go, and how to proceed. To access your super-conscious mind, just like your subconscious, all you need do is command it through thinking the right thoughts.

> You become what you think about.
> **EARL NIGHTINGALE**

> Each time you complete an act of creation, you focus a life force. And since life begets life, this energy seeks to enlarge its expression through new creation. In the stage of completion, your being is ready for another act of creation.
> **ROBERT FRITZ**

> Our attitudes control our lives. Attitudes are a secret power working 24 hours a day, for good or bad. It is of paramount importance that we know how to harness and control this great force.
> **TOM BLANDI**

As Above So Below

Your subconscious, super-conscious, and the universe are totally impartial to your wishes. They simply respond to your energetic intention.

Your thoughts trigger emotions and chemical messengers that together affect the very cells of your being. Thereby your physical body becomes encoded with the vibration of your mind and emotions, and continues to radiate energy like a battery.

Every living thing has an electromagnetic field that is constantly changing, transmitting its energy, and attracting back in like manner.

Aim for success not perfection. Remember that fear always lurks behind perfectionism. Confronting your fears and allowing yourself the right to be human can, paradoxically, make you a far happier and more productive person.
DR. DAVID BURNS

Decree a thing and it shall be established unto thee.
JOB 22:28

I think, therefore I am.
RENÉ DESCARTES

At the time I first came into contact with the philosophy of positive thinking I was blind to the fact that I was quite negative in attitude. After thinking a few positive thoughts for a couple of days, I wondered why I still had negative people and situations showing up in my life, and began to think that the entire philosophy was rubbish. What I needed to learn was that the whole body, not just the mind and emotions, transmits an energy that the universe responds to. Only by maintaining a positive focus for some time was I able to shift the vibration of my thoughts and create a new dominant energy and attraction, hence drawing new people, situations and experience into my life.

It took a personal breakdown for me to experience a *break-through* and see the reality of my situation and myself, and to release the heavy emotional energy that I had been holding onto for so long, which then freed me to move to a higher level.

It is not necessary for you to experience something that extreme before learning the same lesson. All that is required is a willingness to ask these key questions: *What's my motivating energy? Am I coming from fear or love? Is my focus on what's right or wrong; the problem or the solution?*

Principle 7 – Involve to Evolve

We live in an age of great networks, associations and freedom of information. Use it and contribute to it.

The seventh and final rung on the LIFT ladder centres on the consideration of other people when evaluating opportunities, searching for answers, and making decisions about life direction and goals. As with the preceding six principles, this has many aspects and can be applied in several ways. First, ask yourself the question, 'Who do I know that could help me to make this decision, overcome this challenge, or achieve this goal?'

It has never been easier to benefit from the knowledge, experience and wisdom accumulated by others. Books are available that provide specialist advice, experts are offering professional services, and more people have access to the Internet and its vast wealth of information than ever before.

This multidimensional principle also refers to *involving* or turning within yourself, in order to *evolve* or elevate your understanding, by accessing your own inner wisdom.

Try this experience:

> Sit silently by yourself, holding your objective or challenge in mind, and maintain a positive focus.
>
> Keep an upright posture with a straight back and with rhythmic breathing. Breathe in through your nose right down to your stomach, before exhaling out through your mouth.

> In times of change, the learners inherit the earth, while the learned find themselves beautifully equipped to deal with a world that no longer exists.
> **ERIC HOFFER**

> You can never know the answer if you don't ask the question.
> **AUTHOR UNKNOWN**

After one minute of breathing push the tip of your
tongue up to the roof of your mouth. This will
help to activate your right-brain.

In this mental state you are opening your mind to your own inner
wisdom and higher guidance, and should start to receive answers,
insights and ideas. Many people benefit from imagining that they
have a team of advisers, sometimes comprising famous people
from history, who help them reach decisions and find answers.

As a final point and question on this principle, ask yourself, 'If
I make this decision, go down this path, take this opportunity, or
pursue this goal, how will it affect those people who I am already
involved with, such as family, friends, and colleagues?'

The seven principles of LIFT are:

◆ Raise Your Awareness

◆ Develop Possibility Consciousness

◆ Find Balance

◆ Be on Purpose

◆ Become Fully Response-Able

◆ Maintain a Positive Focus

◆ Involve to Evolve

Whether you apply these principles to generate a solution to a
specific situation, or as a guide to your way of being spanning a
lifetime, they stand as timeless guides, and will serve you whatever
your chosen path.

No 1 **Goal Map by Sangeeta**

Focused on: year leading up to 40th birthday

Main Goal (centre) – being at one

Sub Goals (either side of centre) – nurture and grow my family, nurture and grow my career

Why (top images) – greater wellbeing, peace and finding the flow

How (from bottom right) – engage in gardening, writing, and yoga

Who (from bottom left) – by living the qualities of connection, being present, and taking responsibility

No 2 Goal Map by Brian & Sangeeta

Focused on: buying a house

Main Goal (centre) – we have a home of our own

Sub Goals (either side of centre) – our home has an open fire, space, an office, easy connection to main roads

Why (top images) – a sense of nourishment, individualization, putting down roots

How (from bottom right) – find the area and house, arrange the mortgage, exchange contracts

Who (from bottom left) – estate agents, the bank, the solicitor

No 3 **Goal Map by Jane**

Focused on: whole life

Main Goal (centre) – shine like a star

Sub Goals (either side of centre) – wealth, harmony, relationships, and balance

Why (top images) – finding the flow, freedom and peace

How (from bottom right) – creativity, power and focus

Who (from bottom left) – me, Mike, Cynthia

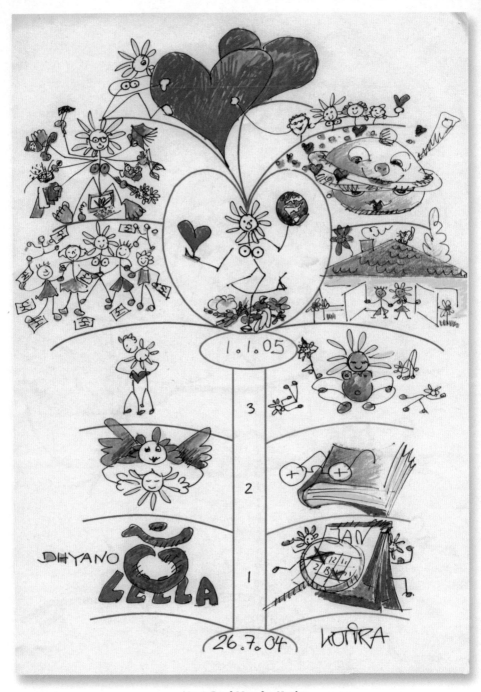

No 4 **Goal Map by Kotira**

Focused on: health and balance

Main Goal (centre) – I am living a healthy lifestyle

Sub Goals (either side of centre) – I love everyone, I live in my own home, I am fully creative, I create success for myself and my friends

Why (top images) – love for my self and my family

How (from bottom right) – focused and disciplined, open to learning, exercise regularly

Who (from bottom left) – Dhyano and Leela, me and my friends

Think about what you want

65

No 5 Goal Map by Brian

Focused on: recycling and going green

Main Goal (centre) – to give back more than is taken

Sub Goals (either side of centre) – recycle waste, reuse building materials, grow our own vegetables, plant trees

Why (top images) – for the next generation, for the planet, for abundance

How (from bottom right) – get separate dustbins, get into the habit, spread the word

Who (from bottom left) – my self, my family, my community

No 6 Goal Map by Jess
Focused on: whole life

Main Goal (centre) – helping my parents enjoy their retirement

Sub Goals (either side of centre) – more show jumping, help parents, advance my career

Why (top images) – happy parents, better life balance, greater freedom

How (from bottom right) – locate new home, develop my brain through reading, create more balance

Who (from bottom left) – friends and colleagues, the local library

No 7 **Goal Map by Chris**

Focused on: creating abundance

Main Goal (centre) – to have the lifestyle of a millionaire

Sub Goals (either side of centre) – play more golf, drive a luxury car, executive box at a football club, regular visits to New York, develop a portfolio of shares

Why (top images) – financial freedom, security and help for children

How (from bottom right) – climb the rope to my goals by being all ears, staying sharp, keeping healthy, building knowledge, making time

Who (from bottom left) – family, teachers, my own intuition

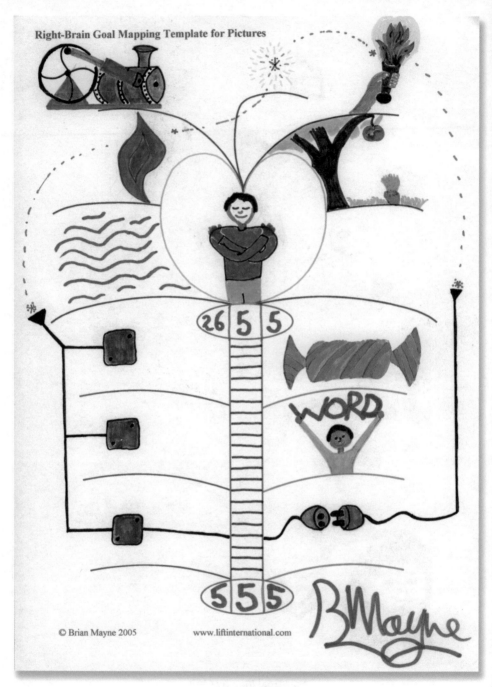

No 8 **Goal Map by Brian**

Focused on: 21 days of wellbeing

Main Goal (centre) – treat my self nicely

Sub Goals (either side of centre) – eat fresh food, breathe clean air, drink pure water, feed my internal flame

Why (top images) – motivation, inspiration, shine an example

How (from bottom right) – focus and connect to my Goal Map, keep my word to my self, choose in the moment

Who (from bottom left) – myself, being my best

Chapter 4

Seven Natural Laws of Manifestation

The seven natural laws of manifestation are like seven signposts pointing the way to success. Follow them and you will arrive at your desired destination. Ignore them and you will end up lost in one of life's ditches.

To manifest is to *bring forth* into clarity, either to the eye or the mind. The manifestations that we bring forth in our life are expressions of our inner thoughts, feelings, and actions. To manifest our conscious intentions we need to ensure that we work with the *natural laws* of creation and *success principles* of the mind.

Seven Laws

The keys to creation.

The principles and laws that govern the process of creation are basic in their nature and few in number. Through the course of this book they have been explored and expanded on in various ways to enable you to understand the foundations on which the

Goal Mapping technique is built. Here the seven laws most fundamental to manifesting your dreams and goals are presented in a concise and succinct manner so as to put you on track for success before embarking on your Goal Mapping journey.

Law 1 – Have Belief in Yourself and Your Goal

Your belief in yourself is like the valve that turns your ability on or off.

On 6 May 1954 Roger Bannister made history by achieving his goal to become the first recorded person in history to run a mile in under 4 minutes. Many people had tried for years to achieve this great feat without success. Leading doctors had stated that it was 'beyond human ability' and it was believed by most to be physically impossible.

What I find truly amazing is that within days of Roger Bannister proving all those doubters wrong, somebody else on the other side of the world called John Landy also broke the 4-minute mile. By the end of 1957, sixteen other people discovered that they could achieve it as well. These days even students in high schools achieve the 4-minute mile. Is it that those following in Bannister's footsteps were fitter or had learnt new techniques? The answer is no. The only thing that had changed following Bannister's success was a newfound belief that the 4-minute mile was possible. Once they believed, it became possible for others to match his achievement.

As explained in Chapter 1, our beliefs are incredibly powerful and affect us mentally, emotionally *and physically*. Each belief that we hold, whether positive or negative, is a thought we have accepted as *true* and that therefore forms a constant command to our subconscious. The longer we hold the belief

> **Never does nature say one thing and wisdom another.**
> **JUVENAL**

> **Nothing splendid has ever been achieved except by those who dared believe that something inside of them was superior to circumstance.**
> **BRUCE BARTON**

> **I am capable of what every other human is capable of. This is one of the great lessons of war and life.**
> **MAYA ANGELOU**

the stronger its emotional energy grows and the deeper ingrained its habit patterns become. Thoughts create feelings, which influence actions. Repeated thoughts accepted as true become beliefs, feelings become attitudes, actions become habits.

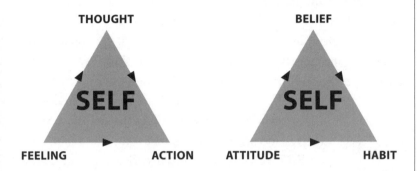

Thought-to-belief cycle

If you set a goal but don't believe you'll achieve it, your limiting belief becomes your 'constant command' and being the stronger, more habitual thought, will probably overpower your new goal-thought. It's as if your goal-thought is a blip in your consciousness, while your limiting belief is the equivalent of a constant groan. As a result your sub-conscious continues to obey your belief and manifest your limitations, rather than hearing your goal-command and desires.

> Man is made by his belief. As he believes, so is he.
> **THE BHAGAVAD GITA**
>
> Under all that we think lives all that we believe, like the ultimate veil to our spirits.
> **ANTONIO MACHADO**

To help your thoughts of success become stronger than any limiting beliefs about failure, it's important to visualize yourself achieving your goals. An intense thought that is repeatedly imagined can't be distinguished from reality by your subconscious. The Goal Mapping technique (see Chapter 6) is designed to help you in this task by empowering your creative right-brain to produce a positive goal image, and reinforce your subconscious thoughts on a daily basis.

Questioning Convictions

Individual greatness stems from our ability to think about our own thinking, and thereby choose our own beliefs.

We observe life through paradigms that filter our perception of reality. In order to build new empowering beliefs and gain the most benefit from your Goal Map it is necessary to dissipate old, limiting and negative beliefs and to avoid making assumptions about people and situations. The more honest your paradigm of your self, other people, and the world around you, the greater your power will be to manifest your desires and achieve your goals.

Each paradigm you hold is like a picture, and each belief is an individual daub of paint that helps to make up the overall image. To bring your paradigms into focus, fine-tune your beliefs by asking yourself the following questions:

◆ Where did I get this belief from in the first place?

◆ Was it my idea or somebody else's opinion?

◆ Was the belief true for me when I adopted it, and is it still true for me now?

◆ Who do I know who is like me and can do that which I believe I can't?

Ask yourself enough questions and you will realize that a limiting belief is only an opinion. If there is nothing of substance to support it, it will simply dissolve away and allow your full power to shine through.

> What lies behind us and what lies before us are tiny matters compared to what lies within us.
>
> **OLIVER WENDELL HOLMES**

> Your chances of success in any undertaking can always be measured by your belief in yourself.
>
> **ROBERT COLLIER**

Law 2 – Balance Your Goals

The first step towards living a balanced life is to set a balance of intentions.

Life is the greatest of all teachers. Each experience, whether a triumph or a tragedy, offers an opportunity to learn. However, we are only able to grasp the gift of learning from any of our failures, and apply it to achieving future goals, if we are emotionally and mentally balanced enough to look at our self and life clearly. Any imbalance leads to a distorted perception that may result in external blame and justification rather than inner *response-ability* and personal power.

Finding balance in your self and life starts by achieving balance in your thinking and emotions; this will help you achieve your goals, which reinforce your life-balance and the process becomes an upward self-enhancing cycle.

The exercise on page 66 has been designed to help you focus on the main areas of your life and to check whether they are in balance. If you haven't completed the exercise already I urge you to do so *now* as it will help you to identify priority goals and achieve maximum balance of the self.

In my own life I make it a rule to engage in a general or *holistic* goal-setting session twice yearly, once in January and again in July; I aim generally to set a balance of goals between:

> When you blame others, you give up your power to change.
> **Dr. Robert Anthony**
>
> Live a balanced life – learn some and think some and draw and paint and sing and dance and play and work every day some.
> **Robert Fulghum**

- ◆ *Personal development goals* – such as new skills or qualities I want to gain.

- ◆ *Career goals* – centring on my professional ability and work success.

- ◆ *Financial goals* – around levels of income, savings or investments.

◆ *Heath and fitness goals* – that centre on diet, cleansing and exercise.

◆ *Toy and adventure goals* – such as places I want to visit and rewards I choose to give to myself.

◆ *Quality of life goals* – that encompass home and family life are decided together with my wife.

I use the balance exercise (see page 66) to identify any flat areas: these become the priority areas for focus in order to bring my life into balance. Not only does this process help me to achieve a good state of balance, it also keeps my life interesting and makes it work well.

> Sometimes when I consider what tremendous consequences come from little things ... I am tempted to think ... there are no little things.
> **BRUCE BARTON**

Balancing Time

Short-, medium- and long-term goals all lead to fulfilment of your dreams.

When aiming to achieve balance in your life and your goals it is important to give consideration to the balance of time spent across each area. Set a mixture of long-term, medium-term, and short-term goals. The achievement of a simple short-term goal provides encouragement and a boost in self-belief, enabling you to move more easily to the next goal. Short-term goals can be achieved in just a few hours or days, medium-term goals in weeks or months, and long-term goals take a year or more.

If you have an *ongoing* objective, with no end date, then that isn't really a goal at all – it's a purpose or life-path. In order to make progress towards achieving an ongoing objective it's a good idea to set many smaller goals along the way that act like milestones.

> Nothing is particularly hard if you divide it into small jobs.
> **HENRY FORD**

Helping it Happen

Find balance between making it happen, and letting it happen. 'Help' it to happen.

Finally, for this particular law to work, seek balance in the approach you take towards the achievement of your goals. In all acts of manifestation look to achieve balance between *making* things happen and *letting* things happen. If you are overly strong or egotistical in forcing a goal into existence you may end up creating something that proves to be detrimental or unsustainable in some way, because you will be pushing against the natural flow. If you are too passive and sit back waiting for the goal to happen you may end up waiting a very long time, as there will not be sufficient energy generated to encourage its actualisation.

The key, and balance point, is to *help* your goal to happen. The universe knows the best time and way for your goals to be actualized. Know that the universe is working with you, and find the flow by setting your intentions in the following balanced affirmation:

> Let your heart guide you. It whispers, so listen closely.
> **THE LAND BEFORE TIME**

'If it be for my highest good and the highest good of all, then... [state your goals].'

Stay focused upon your goals, knowing they already exist at some level, and that your task is to draw them into physical reality through thought, word and deed. The key is to proceed with the energy of desire, not need.

Law 3 – Live in The Moment

Learn from the past, visualize the future, be present in the now.

It is said that *energy flows where attention goes.* When your attention is in the past, you and your energy are in the past.

> Live for the present, dream of the future, learn from the past.
> **AUTHOR UNKNOWN**

> The best time to plant a tree was 20 years ago. The second best time is now.
> **CHINESE PROVERB**

> The power of memories and expectations is such that for most human beings the past and the future are not as real, but rather more real than the present.
> **ALAN WATTS**

When your attention is in the future, you and your energy are in the future. However it is when you are focused in the *present moment* that you connect with the real power of the universe and manifest your desires.

It is important to examine the past as that's one of the main ways we learn the lessons of life. Likewise it is absolutely vital to visualize our future, as that is the first step towards creating it, but we must place the majority of our focus in the *now*, especially when seeking to manifest our desires, because this is where creation exists. The present has power.

Everything that takes place happens in the moment of *now*. All of your memories were once 'now' moments, and your future is made up of 'now' moments that are to come. Being fully present in the current moment gives you the opportunity to create great memories and plant healthy seeds for the future that will grow into tomorrow's harvest.

Unfortunately, some people become trapped in the past because they can't let go of old mistakes, grievances, or come to terms with opportunities that have slipped them by. Others become fixed on the future and set rules for themselves as to when they can be happy. Their general mindset is, 'I'll be happy when I get the promotion, achievement, or right person in my life.' However, happiness is a *now* experience, it happens in the moment of now, not then. Learning to be happy with whatever you have in your life in the moment of *now* creates the right energy of gratitude to help you to achieve your goals. The ancient Sanskrit poem below puts it beautifully:

Look well to this day, for it is life, the very best of life.

In its brief course lay all the realities and truths of existence – The joys of growth, the splendour of action, the glory of power.

For yesterday is but a memory, and tomorrow is only a vision.

But today, if well lived, makes every yesterday a memory of happiness, and every tomorrow a vision of hope.

Look well to this day.

This fine piece of wisdom was discovered carved into a clay tablet in the ruins of ancient Babylon around 4,500 years ago. It is as true today as it was then and will still be true in another 4,500 years time. It represents the fundamental truth that though situations and circumstance will change constantly, certain truths are timeless. The truth of this principle is that all creation lives in the now and we must be present in the moment if we are to be at our best and achieve our true desires.

Law 4 – State Your Goals in Present Tense

The past is history, tomorrow is a mystery, today is a gift – that's why they call it the present.

There are many interpretations that can be applied to living in the now; at the most basic level it means simply *paying attention*, *being present*, and being *fully connected*. One of the best ways of achieving this is to state your goals, and anchor your intentions in *present tense* language.

> Don't let what you cannot do interfere with what you can do.
> **John Wooden**

Stating your goals in present tense is essential for conscious manifestation because creation always exists in the moment of now. Likewise it is only in the moment of now that you can be truly *response-able*. If you choose your response based on your past you are being *re-active*. Choosing how you want to respond in the future is *pro-active*. But it's only by living in the *now* that you gain the ideal, natural response that unfolds and flows in the moment.

Making it Real

Turning thoughts into things.

> Realize that now, in this moment of time, you are creating. You are creating your next moment. That is what's real.
>
> **SARA PADDISON**

> Be happy in the moment, that's enough. Each moment is all we need, not more.
>
> **MOTHER TERESA**

> There is surely nothing other than the single purpose of the present moment. A man's whole life is a succession of moment after moment. If one fully understands the present moment, there will be nothing else to do, and nothing else to pursue.
>
> **HAGAKURE**

At a macro level the universe exists in the moment, and so it is at a micro level in our individual subconscious and super-conscious mind. Time exists in our conscious mind as a way of separating *now* moments into past, present, and future. But our subconscious doesn't work that way; the subconscious like the universe lives in the moment and responds to now.

Many people fall into the trap of stating their goals in future tense, which means that in the future is where the goals stay. This happens unintentionally, but by using left-brain thinking and the conscious mind they rationalize that if they haven't achieved their goals yet then their wishes must begin: 'I want to', 'I will do' or, 'I intend and plan to'. The challenge with these statements and others like them is that they place your goal in the future, while your subconscious intent lives in the now.

If you state a goal or intention such as: '*I want to* be happy or healthy, or wealthy', what you actually achieve is *wanting*. You'll wake up tomorrow *wanting* to be happy, or healthy or wealthy; the day after that you'll *achieve* 'wanting', and so it will continue because your statement will always keep your goal at arms' length.

Your subconscious has an underlying commitment to make you and your life fit your dominant thoughts and beliefs. If you *think* you can do something, your subconscious will take that thought as a command and start working on it. However, it's not thinking you can do something *in the future* that creates personal power, it's visualizing yourself achieving it as if you are living it *now* that commands your subconscious into action.

Anchoring the Dream

Transforming visualization into actualization.

Stating in the moment has long been a practice of various spiritual groups who chant their awareness, or tell themselves what they are doing constantly in order to keep the mind focused. Likewise, if you practise visualization, the key is to see yourself living your goal as if it already exists and has been achieved: see it, say it, feel it, taste it, smell it. You'll then come to believe it, causing your subconscious to respond quickly and achieve it.

Law 5 – State Your Goals in Positive Tense

Your word is your wand; wield it with wisdom.

We maintain our focus and create our world by *thought, word* and *deed*. All thought energy is creative and attractive, but a thought associated with strong feelings that is spoken aloud takes on a much denser vibration and increases in power. When the spoken thought and feeling are acted upon they become more powerful still. No-one is more powerful than someone who speaks their mind and then does what they say. In contrast, duplicitous two-faced people who don't speak their mind and don't act as they speak are generally despised, and diminish their own power.

Your language is a reflection of your mindset; your mindset a reflection of your dominant thoughts and beliefs; your dominant thoughts and beliefs are the constant commands to your super and subconscious. To enable yourself to hold a positive thought, generating true power, and commanding the universe, it is important to adopt a positive vocabulary, and keep the integrity between your thoughts, feelings, words and actions.

> As we express our gratitude, we must never forget that the highest appreciation is not to utter words, but to live by them.
> **JOHN F. KENNEDY**

Mind Your Language

See and say things as you want them to be.

Early in my training career I set a goal to improve my memory and decided to learn memory techniques. The first step was to examine my own thoughts and comments and to stop saying to myself: 'I have a terrible memory'. I also needed to stop commanding other people in a negative way, saying things such as, *'Don't forget'*, when what I really meant was, *'Please remember'*.

> We tend to get what we expect.
> **NORMAN VINCENT PEALE**
>
> We should not let our fears hold us back from pursuing our hopes.
> **JOHN F. KENNEDY**

It's easy to fall into the trap of giving unconscious negative commands. I work currently with a couple of child therapists who spend the majority of their time working not with the child, but with the parents. Young children are particularly susceptible to comments that are made to them because they haven't built up a sufficiently strong sense of self (conscious mind) to question, and their subconscious takes the command literally. If you ever doubt the power of suggestion, ask yourself what happens when you say to a child 'Don't touch!' The chances are the child will immediately touch whatever it is you want them to avoid. Likewise, telling a child repeatedly, not to be 'so clumsy, stupid or lazy', results only in producing exactly those negative outcomes. Remember your subconscious cannot make value judgements (see page 10). This means that, 'Don't *do it*' emphasizes 'do it', and 'No *more*' is understood to mean '*more*'.

Check your own self-talk for negative comments and subconscious commands. You may know in your conscious mind that you don't really want to follow them, but unless you change them for positive supporting statements, they will continue to be subconscious commands and hold you back.

Positive Thinking

Look for what's best – in your self, in your life, in others – and you'll find it.

Positive thinking is not about being happy just for the sake of it (although that's a good idea and a worthy goal) nor does it mean ignoring the negative. (If you're blind to the pit-falls in life you'll end up tumbling down the pit). Positive thinking is a strategy for finding your best way forward, towards lasting happiness, peace and plenty; it is a success technique for spotting opportunity in difficulty, the silver lining in the storm cloud.

Whatever goal we focus on grows in our awareness and, through the law of attraction, moves us closer towards it. In focusing on the problem you will find more of the problem but if you focus on the solution to the problem you move towards that goal instead. Look for what's right in your self, and you'll boost your self-esteem and build your self-confidence. Look for what's right in your life and you'll spot opportunities and find solutions. Look for what's right in other people and you'll create harmony, peace and synergy.

It's important to reiterate that you must state what you want, not what you fear.

This may sound obvious but the reality is that many people set negative goals and intentions without realizing what they are doing. The classic example relates to smoking. When I first set a goal to give up smoking I made the mistake of stating it in negative terms: 'I don't want to smoke any more.'

The goal and statement actually created a thought picture of me *smoking more, while not really wanting to smoke* and that's exactly the result I got: two weeks later I found myself smoking more than ever, and being really fed up about it. I reset my goal, this time seeking to use a purely positive term for not

> Don't find fault, find a remedy.
> **HENRY FORD**

> Problems are what you see when you take your eye off your goals.
> **BRIAN TRACY**

> The indispensable first step to getting the things you want out of life is this: decide what you want.
> **BEN STEIN**

smoking. All I could come up with was, 'I'm an air breather', which although true and positive, was so weak that it had little impact.

It required me to dig deep within myself to become really clear about what I wanted. I wanted to be free of my addiction, but I also wanted to be free in a general sense – free to choose – to smoke if I wanted to and to not smoke if I didn't want to. Once I set my goal in positive terms and in the present tense as a goal statement: '*I am free*', the addiction simply started to dissipate.

Law 6 – State Your Goals in Personal Tense.

You can set goals only for yourself, not for anyone else.

In order for any goal to work at either a subconscious or super-conscious level, it must be something that you believe in personally, and the goal must therefore be set by you. You really can't set goals for, or about, anyone else, just as nobody else can set goals for you. You are the master of your subconscious 'genie' and your genie will work only for you.

I often encounter people who are resistant towards the idea of setting goals because they've had the idea forced upon them at some point in their past and may have had no say in the sorts of goals to be set. Chances are that a well-meaning parent, teacher, or boss has said: 'Here's what you need to do, so set a goal and go for it.'

Many years ago I made the mistake of setting a goal to marry a certain person. It wasn't her goal, only mine, it didn't happen. In like manner I'm sometimes asked in my workshops: 'How can I change my husband/wife?' Well you can try getting a new husband or wife, but you're not going to change the person. People change when they want to.

In my corporate work I've witnessed managers

> It is not the mountain we conquer but ourselves.
> **SIR EDMUND HILLARY**

> Always bear in mind, that your own resolution to succeed is more important than any other thing.
> **ABRAHAM LINCOLN**

announcing the latest goal to their team, not realizing that the *goal* is only their goal or company's objective. It will not become the team's goal until the team takes some form of ownership. That happens when each individual member steps forward and commits themselves to it.

Somebody else may identify the target, but unless you buy into it personally, it doesn't become your goal in a true sense. We each have our own free will; we each create and live our own reality; we each have our very own personal subconscious 'genie' to help us achieve this; and each of us is personally response-able for what we command our subconscious towards.

> **Individual commitment to a group effort – that is what makes a team work, a company work, a society work, a civilization work.**
>
> **VINCE LOMBARDI**

Law 7 – Allow for Lag-Time

Own the gap between thought and creation.

Think about what happens when you blink your eyes. The gap of time between thinking the thought and achieving the result is comparatively short (unless you are over-riding the thought with another and commanding your eyes to stay open). The lag-time between the setting of your goal and achieving it will be determined more by the strength of your belief and consistency of conviction than by your physical circumstances and personal ability. In simple terms the most fundamental requirement in achieving any goal is to make the thought of you achieving, stronger than the thought of you failing.

All goals are relative. What might be a big goal to you may be a small goal to someone else, or vice versa. A big goal means simply that it is far beyond where you are currently in your life and your self, which means you will need to grow, both in terms of self-belief and physical ability. It's your *belief* that takes priority because belief regulates *physical ability*.

Some years ago when I set the goal to teach myself to read

and write well, I gave myself twelve months to achieve my objective, and it took twelve months. In conjunction with the goal of learning to read, I decided to set the goal of writing a book, so as to have a measurable benchmark of my achievement. For this I gave myself eighteen months, figuring that if it took twelve months to learn to read, it would take another six to write the book.

Eighteen months came and went… and no book. At first I became disheartened, and even went to the extent of blaming and moaning that goal-setting didn't work. Then I remembered what one of my mentors had taught me: 'Brian, when things don't turn out as you'd planned, give yourself a *check-up, from the neck up*. Check your point of mental focus first and foremost to ensure that your paradigm of the situation is honest, accurate and clear, before you become fixated on the details.

Once I chose to focus on what was right I became aware that I'd achieved quite a lot in the time-span; I needed simply to reset the goal of the book. Again I gave myself eighteen months and again eighteen months passed with no sign of the book. As before I fell into the trap of becoming negative, but only for a short time. I soon gave myself the check-up, focused on the positive, and recognized that during the allotted period I had developed my writing ability and had several articles published; so I chose to re-set the goal again.

In total it took over four years to achieve the goal of a published book. However it's important to bear in mind that it wasn't the only thing that I worked on during that time. It actually took a relatively small amount of my effort to achieve. What really took four years was not the physical activity, but building my belief that I could do it.

> I do not think there is any other quality so essential to success of any kind as the quality of perseverance. It overcomes almost everything, even nature.
>
> **JOHN D. ROCKEFELLER**

> The only thing that stands between a man and what he wants from life is often merely the will to try it and the faith to believe that it is possible.
>
> **RICHARD M. DEVOS**

Draw Your Bow

It is thy right and thy might.

Setting a goal is like firing an arrow: the more ambitious the goal the longer the arrow will take to reach its target. The first step is for the archer to decide where to aim by setting a goal. Next the archer must muster strength to draw the bow, or create a powerful thought picture that becomes dominant. Finally the archer releases the arrow and waits the *lag-time* for it to hit the target.

Regardless of the type or size of your goal, make sure that you allow for the lag time between visualization and actualization; many people don't afford their genie-subconscious sufficient time to work their magic.

If you've spent years talking to yourself negatively or holding a limiting belief, it will take a little while to build the power of your positive intentions and make them dominant. The more often that you set and review your goals, the more their power will grow, and the faster your subconscious will work to achieve them. No matter how long it takes, stay true to your dream. Review and restate your goals regularly, and remember to allow for lag-time.

> This one step, choosing a goal and sticking to it, changes everything.
> **SCOTT REED**

> The future belongs to those who believe in the beauty of their dreams.
> **ELEANOR ROOSEVELT**

Chapter 5

Preparation for Manifestation

True preparation for a meaningful goal requires everything that has gone in the pages before. It can take a lifetime to apply logically or a heart-beat to flow naturally.

Mental Preparation

Who you choose to be as a person empowers the things you do and leads to what you have.

In order to flow naturally towards the achievement of your goals, working in harmony with the fundamental laws of creation, it is important to honour the natural order of success: to *Be*, before you *Do*, in order to *Have*.

The manifestation of any goal or thing we want to *have* is always achieved more by who we are *being* than by what we are physically *doing*. Whether the task is relatively mundane, requiring a low level of skill and knowledge, or a specialized activity with higher levels of skills and knowledge, it is still our

> The meeting of preparation with opportunity generates the offspring we call luck.
> **ANTHONY ROBBINS**

way of *being* – such as enthusiastic, considerate, or courageous – that will determine not only the quantity of goals we achieve but also the quality.

Drive, Attitude, Confidence: the DAC Factor

Riding the bike of ability.

Imagine that your regular activity, whether your work, hobby or daily responsibility, is like riding a bicycle.

The back wheel of the bike represents your technical knowledge and skill sets. Without it your bike isn't going to go anywhere. From the moment we enter school we begin to learn skills and accumulate technical knowledge. As we progress through school our knowledge and skills become more and more focused as we home in on our choice of career. When we leave school and go onto higher education or into an occupation, the scope of our technical knowledge and skill becomes even more refined.

Regardless of what you do on a daily basis, and irrespective of your qualifications, the chances are that you have amassed a high level of specific knowledge that enables you to achieve results in your regular activities; to the extent that, if you were to ask me to take over your duties for the day I'd probably be lost until I had gained some of your technical knowledge and skills. The more specialized your chosen occupation or activity, the more specific your knowledge and skills will need to be. However, regardless of level, everyone must have a back wheel if their bike is to make any progress in life.

What is the main function of the front wheel of a bike? To *steer*. Your front wheel is your steering mechanism: your ability to communicate and to influence. The front wheel represents

> Confidence...thrives only on honesty, on honour, on the sacredness of obligations, on faithful protection and on unselfish performance. Without them, it cannot live.
> **FRANKLIN D. ROOSEVELT**

> There are no secrets to success. It is the result of preparation, hard work, and learning from failure.
> **COLIN POWELL**

your social skills, which develop over a long period of time.

The bike is an analogy for whatever you do: the back wheel represents your technical knowledge and the front wheel your people skills, but make no mistake it is YOU that gets up every morning and pedals the bike.

Some days we pedal really hard at the thing we've chosen to do, and other days we don't feel the same way and look for some flat ground or even a slope to coast down. What makes the difference between the days we pedal hard and the days we coast stems from three core qualities of character, known as the DAC factor:

◆ Drive

◆ Attitude

◆ Confidence

Your ability to develop and call upon good levels of DAC will be the major factor determining how successful you are in whatever you choose to focus on, in whatever aspect of your life.

A young student pointed out to me recently that drive, attitude and confidence determine not just how well you power the back wheel of your bike, but how much you develop the wheel in the first place. If you learn DAC when young you see the value of education and make the most of it; if you don't, you will coast wherever possible and drop out as soon as you can. Progress in life does not relate so much to the terrain we're crossing, as to who we are *being* when we ride.

> Character is to the quality of man, what carbon is to steel.
> **AUTHOR UNKNOWN**

Becoming More

The ongoing master goal for each of us is to evolve and be our best.

Each of the three core qualities of *drive* (being able to motivate your self), *attitude* (the ability to maintain a positive focus) and *confidence* (authentic self-belief), empowers you to achieve your goals; the qualities are further developed through the process of goal-setting. Having a goal, a sense of direction or a compelling purpose, generates motivation and provides momentum, thereby producing stability in life. It is the pursuit of goals that causes us to stretch ourselves, focus on solutions, and gain confidence, by stepping outside of our comfort zone.

When we honour the prime principle of 'becoming more' in life our physical goals become the outward reflection of our inner greatness. When we violate the principle, no amount of external success will ever compensate for our inner failings.

One of the great challenges in the western world is that we often distort the natural urge to *become more* into a belief that happiness is achieved through *having more*: more money, a bigger house, a faster car. This paradigm is a source of much misery. The satisfaction gained in achieving these things will be short-lived unless they are balanced by the achievement of self-development. In preparing to achieve any goal it is of prime importance to make sure you are *being* the person who would achieve that goal.

> **The journey is the reward.**
> **TAOIST PROVERB**
>
> **Self-conquest is the greatest of victories.**
> **PLATO**

Physical Preparation

Making good your plans for tomorrow.

The effectiveness of any type of goal-setting technique, whether focused on achieving *things*, or developing *qualities of character*, will be determined by the ability to connect your conscious objectives to your subconscious. The main path to your subconscious is through your right-brain and your right-brain thinks in pictures.

Everyone, at some level, thinks in pictures even if they don't always realize it. Many people think mistakenly that they don't visualize because they don't see clear, bright, colourful images.

But this doesn't mean that they're not thinking in pictures or imagining.

For many people, pictures that flash through their mind are so fleeting, and sometimes at such a high level, that they are completely unaware of them. However, you need only to lie back, relax, and close your eyes, for pictures of your thoughts to start to drift into your consciousness.

Do you dream in words or pictures? It's always pictures. You may hear words in your dream, just as you may hear yourself thinking, but the words are always reflections of the thought pictures. It is for this reason that Goal Mapping uses a combination of words and imagery to fully activate your whole-brain and form a deep connection to your subconscious.

Before continuing with the next chapter and creating your first Goal Map, there are a few things you will need to gather and prepare to maximize the power of your Map. The most important factor is the preparation of your Goal Mapping templates.

In the appendix to this book you will find both the left-brain and right-brain Goal Mapping templates, which are best photocopied, redrawn onto A4 or A3 card, or downloaded free from www.goalmapping.com. Using copies will allow you to use the templates again, and means also that your finished Goal Map is not tied to this book.

> The greatest unexplored territory in the world is the space between our ears.
> **BILL O'BRIEN**
>
> Part of success is preparation on purpose.
> **JIM ROHN**

I strongly recommend using templates for your first couple of Goal Maps as they will help you stay true to the seven steps intrinsic to the technique. However, once you are familiar with the process you'll soon find that you can create your Maps from scratch using just a blank sheet of paper.

As colour is a strong right-brain stimulant I also encourage you to use coloured pens (I like the fibre tip ones best) together with a pencil, pen, rubber and ruler.

Give yourself some quiet, undisturbed time for the creation of your first Goal Map; allow a minimum of an hour, although you'll find drawing subsequent Maps much quicker.

If possible, arrange to create your Map in a tranquil nurturing space; but if that is not possible, use the relaxation exercises on page 111 to create a calm space inside your head.

Finally, music is another excellent right-brain stimulant and many people benefit from playing mood-enhancing music at low volume in the background while Goal Mapping. Make sure it's something easy and soft that will calm and inspire you.

> **Music is the interstate highway to the memory system.**
> TERRY WYLER WEBB

Part Two

The Goal
Mapping
Technique

Chapter 6

Creating Your Goal Map

To be the architect of a great life, you must first envisage, and then create, a great plan.

Re-Mind

Knowing the story.

Positive thinking is the foundation stone on which the Goal Mapping technique rests. It represents the process of change and conscious creation, without which your ability for purposeful manifestation is severally reduced.

We now know that:

◆ For better or worse, richer or poorer, we each have a hand in shaping our life.

◆ The primary *cause* that creates the *effects*, or personal circumstances of our life, is our *thoughts*.

◆ While some people think consistently about what they want, many more focus regularly on what they fear, and that which you choose to focus upon, your subconscious starts to create.

The key to why things change is the key to everything.
JAMES BURKE

As a man thinketh in his heart, so is he.
PROVERBS 23.7

A Way Forward

With the summary points in mind, it would seem obvious that to create any form of success we must first create a *dominant thought command* about it.

Some of you may be thinking as I used to: 'Why not simply sit down, with my eyes closed, and visualize or hold a *thought* about my goals? Could I think that thought with intensity for about thirty minutes, so as to make it the *dominant goal* for my subconscious to follow?'

The reason 'why not' is because it's extremely difficult to hold your mind on just one thought. Generally, people become distracted, uncomfortable or sleepy after only a few minutes. The mind drifts and before they know it, they've lost their focus.

However, by engaging in the following seven steps of Goal Mapping the very process of moving through the steps themselves, writing and drawing your physical Goal Map results in creating a mirror image or thought-picture in your mind: a new dominant *goal command* for your subconscious genie to pursue.

> **Thinking is the hardest work there is, which is the probable reason why so few engage in it.**
> **HENRY FORD**
>
> **Never begin the day until it is finished on paper.**
> **JIM ROHN**

Seven Steps of Goal Mapping

The thumbprint of manifestation.

The seven steps of Goal Mapping are:

◆ **Dream**   *'What do I want?'*

◆ **Order**   *'What's my priority?'*

◆ **Draw**   *'What does it look like?'*

◆ **Why**   *'Why do I want it?'*

◆ **When** *'When do I want it?'*

◆ **How** *'How will I achieve it?'*

◆ **Who** *'Whose help will I require?'*

The seven steps are intrinsic aspects in any form of conscious creation. That is, anyone seeking to achieve anything will need to action the seven steps in one way or another because they represent the vital questions of success, such as: *'What* do you want?'; *'What's the priority?'*; *'Why* do you want it?'; *'When* by?'; *'How* will you do it?'; and *'Who* will be involved?'

Asking yourself these questions and acting on the answers is essential for any form of conscious manifestation. The Goal Mapping technique is designed to guide you through these stages of planning for success and capture your answers in both a written and visual Map, which then acts as a conscious reminder, and reinforces your subconscious command.

> Reduce your plan to writing... The moment you complete this, you will have definitely given concrete form to the intangible desire.
>
> **NAPOLEON HILL**

By engaging in the process of creating your Goal Map you will live the principles of positive thinking and focus on what you want. Afterwards the ritual of *living your Goal Map* on a daily basis will maintain your subconscious command, and foster a conscious demonstration of your faith in yourself, your belief in your goals, and your commitment to your dreams.

Picture Power

Make a stand for your future by cementing your intentions on paper.

To gain the power of Goal Mapping you need to engage in creating one; it is not enough to just *know* about the technique. Some people, myself amongst them in the past, profess to *know* what they want, and feel no need to declare it physically in the form of a goal. However, holding what you want in your head doesn't equal the power of defining it and stating it on paper. Thoughts can be fleeting and the mind deceiving.

The process of manifestation in any form always involves raising the energy of your desires. Make sure that your thoughts of success are boosted higher than your fears of failure. If you set your intentions for your future down on paper, you'll be birthing a thought form that, through the law of attraction, will reach out into the universe, rather like casting out your net into an ocean of potential.

> If you are failing to plan you are planning to fail.
> **BRIAN TRACY**

Step 1. Dream

What do you want?

The first step of setting any intention is to *Dream*. It's a purely right-brain function. Your right-brain looks forward with the gift of imagination and visualization. Activating your right-brain allows you to '*see what you want*' and hence begin your journey towards it.

There are many ways to activate your right-brain and most of them involve some form of relaxation and change in breathing. If you already have a favourite technique use it, otherwise simply follow on below.

Relax

Free your mind to find the flow.

◆ Sit in a comfortable upright position with your back straight and your bottom pushed against the rear of the chair. Put your feet flat on the floor, with your hands in your lap, palms up.

◆ Take a deep breath in through your nose, and

> Nothing happens unless first a dream.
> **CARL SANBERG**
>
> When we are unable to find tranquillity within ourselves, it is useless to seek it elsewhere.
> **KENNETH PRATT**

hold it; without letting it go, inhale a second time, so that your breath goes all the way down to your stomach. Wait a moment, before breathing out slowly through your mouth while saying the word 'RELAX' to yourself, three times.

◆ Repeat the breathing exercise, this time saying the words 'I AM', three times.

◆ Repeat once more, while saying the word, 'WITHIN', three times.

◆ Your command to your self is: 'RELAX – I AM – WITHIN'

It feels safe and pleasant to be completely relaxed. I'd like you to imagine a stream of relaxation flowing in through the top of your head that gradually relaxes all the areas of your body. Maybe you could picture this relaxation energy as *white light*.

◆ Imagine what it would feel like to really *relax* your *scalp, forehead, ears, tongue,* and *jaw*. Give yourself permission *now* to relax those areas completely; allowing them to become more and more gently relaxed as we continue.

◆ Now imagine this relaxing white light flowing down through your *neck, shoulders, arms* and *hands*. Give yourself permission to relax *those* areas completely, allowing them to become more gently relaxed with each easy breath that you take.

◆ This soothing relaxation now seeps down through your *chest*, gradually relaxing all your *inner organs*, before reaching your *hips, thighs, calves, ankles, feet* and *toes*. A gentle wave of white-light relaxation flows softly through your entire body, tenderly soothing and nourishing every cell.

> Nowhere can man find a quieter or more untroubled retreat than in his own soul.
> **MARCUS AURELIUS**

◆ Next, lightly push the tip of your tongue against the roof of your mouth for a moment, and imagine yourself strolling along a beautiful sandy sea shore. A clear blue sky is above you, with just a few white fluffy clouds. Trees sway gently in a warm summer breeze, waves ripple softly against the shoreline and you feel the texture of the wet sand as it squishes up between your toes.

◆ As you walk along this safe and relaxing shore, your attention is drawn suddenly to a small blue bottle poking slightly from the sand. When you pick up the bottle the top comes open, and to your amazement there appears in front of you a large blue shinning eyed *genie*.

◆ The genie says, 'Your wish is my command. Any "thing" that you truly desire I will obey. Any "thought" that you hold in your heart I will help you achieve.'

I want you now to take your self forward in time knowing you have the power to create your life exactly as you would choose it to be.

> **The one without dreams is the one without wings.**
> **MUHAMMAD ALI**
>
> **Only in imagination does every truth find an effective and undeniable existence. Imagination is the supreme master of life.**
> **JOSEPH CONRAD**

Ask yourself:

◆ What does success look like for me?

◆ What are some of the important areas of my life?

◆ What are the major activities that make my day?

◆ What type of home am I living in and where is it?

◆ What style of car do I drive?

◆ What kind of work do I choose?

◆ Who are the people around me?

Really get in touch with your picture, and then notice how it feels to be living your life at your best.

◆ Who are you *being* as a person? What are some of the major emotions and qualities you experience when seeing yourself achieve your dreams?

◆ *See* all the sights. *Hear* all the sounds. *Feel* all the feelings, and remember the key principle of conscious creation: 'Whatever you can *conceive* and *believe*, you can work towards and ultimately *achieve*.'

Close your eyes to visualize for a moment now, and when you are ready return to the present bringing with you any insight, intention, or desire that empowers you.

Please use the visualization exercise above before going further.

Now quickly capture your insights in the spaces below. Use short statements. Just record the essence for now, even a single KEY WORD will do, you can add more detail later.

The universe is change; our life is what our thoughts make it.

MARCUS AURELIUS

Make no small plans for they have not the power to stir men's blood.

NICCOLÒ MACHIAVELLI

Be not afraid of life. Believe that life is worth living, and your belief will help create the fact.

HENRY JAMES

My Vision for My Future is:

. . . .

. . . .

. . . .

. . . .

. . . .

. . . .

. . . .

. . . .

> We grow through our dreams. All great men and women are dreamers. Some, however, allow their dreams to die. You should nurse your dreams and protect them through bad times and tough times to the sunshine and light which always come.
> **WOODROW WILSON**

. . . .

. . . .

. . . .

Step 1: Dream

How many of the above spaces have you filled?

Ideally, to allow for balance and choice, I would like you to have listed at least five or more goals covering different life areas. At a minimum you require at least three goals, but if you can really only think of one, then continue with that. If you have existing goals that you are already working on, add them to your list now. Let your mind run free. Approach the exercise as if everything were possible. If you are going to dream – practise dreaming big.

Some people become conditioned in childhood to believe that it's a waste of time to daydream, but some of the greatest achievers in history have been dreamers and some of the greatest achievements came about through dreaming.

Einstein was considered a dreamy child who didn't learn to speak until comparatively late. His parents were told that he didn't have the mental capacity for an academic career and that he was better suited to trade school. However, his greatest breakthrough, when working on the theory of relativity, came to him while daydreaming about what it would be like to ride a beam of light to the end of the universe.

> A rock pile ceases to be a rock pile the moment a single man contemplates it, bearing with him the image of a cathedral.
>
> **ANTOINE DE SAINT-EXUPÉRY**

Knowing What You Want

Lifting the fog of fear.

Occasionally, someone on my workshop will experience their mind going blank just at the point of setting some goals. There can be a number of reasons for this but usually it comes down to some sort of fear. It happened to me the first time I was confronted with a goal-setting exercise.

I remember sitting with a completely blank mind and an equally blank sheet of paper. In that moment I really couldn't think of anything that I wanted. It took my mentor to point out that I was almost £1,000,000 in debt, with no home, no qualifications, and unable to read or write properly. 'Surely there

> Imagination is more important than knowledge.
>
> **ALBERT EINSTEIN**

must be something that you want?' he questioned.

Of course there were many things: some practical, some essential, and others that were purely pleasurable. But I didn't have the belief that I'd actually be able to achieve any of them. To protect myself from disappointment I was telling myself there was nothing I really wanted, which was very convenient as it meant I wouldn't need to go outside my comfort zone and face the fear of failing.

Once I realized that I was blocking myself because of fear, the fog in my mind began slowly to lift and a vision of an empowering future started to form. It took a little while to exercise my goal-setting muscles of belief and imagination, but before long I started stretching myself with some adventurous and truly empowering goals.

If you are experiencing any difficulty with this first step simply sit quietly for a moment and listen to what your heart has to say, instead of your head. While your head may be foggy, rambling round in circles, or trying to justify something that is neither possible nor realistic, your heart will always speak true and clear.

Check yourself for any fears that may be holding you back, accept them as being there to protect you in some way, and then choose to move beyond them by stating your intentions in the form of an inspiring goal.

If at this point you still don't know what you want, ask yourself if you know what you *don't* want, and then write down the positive opposite.

> Vision is the art of seeing things invisible.
> **JONATHAN SWIFT**

> The mind is a mansion but most of the time we are content to live in the lobby.
> **DR WILLIAM MICHAELS**

> The greatest human temptation is to settle for too little.
> **THOMAS MERTON**

Step 2. Order

What's the priority?

Step 1 involved you in dreaming by thinking with your right-brain so as to create a vision of your future. Step 2 *Order*, requires you to action your left-brain and work out which of your goals is the most important.

Often people will say that they want all of their goals equally, that they are *all* really important; and this may well be true. However experience shows that there is always *one* goal that when achieved automatically helps towards the achievement of the others.

A simple example of this may be that your goals are:

> Let all things be done decently and in order.
> CORINTHIANS 14.40
>
> Things which matter most must never be at the mercy of things that matter least.
> GOETHE

◆ To go on a dream holiday.

◆ To gain a promotion in your work.

◆ To move to a bigger home.

In this example the promotion would become the main goal, as its achievement would supply the resources to help the other two goals to happen. The above is just an example and the priorities will be slightly different for everyone, however it represents the essence of the principle.

Another common example comes from my Goal Mapping sessions with students, where they realize that their *education* is the main goal that will then help them to get the job of their choice and the lifestyle they desire.

Ask yourself the question now: 'Which one of my goals when achieved will automatically help me to achieve the others?'

Once you've decided, turn to the left-brain Goal Mapping template on page 170 and write your goal in the central box marked Main Goal. (If you do not want to write in the book, photocopy the page or download extra copies from our website.) Use a maximum of ten words, making sure you state your goal in alignment with the *fundamental laws of manifestation*, writing in *positive*, *personal*, and *present* tense.

Do This Now

There is a power in getting to the essence of your goal. There is no wisdom in waffle. Work to reduce your goal statement to as few words as possible and you will find the absolute core of your intention, and be better able to internalise it. See the left-brain example on page 170 for ways in which to express this.

Now select four more goals from the list you compiled on page 115. Ideally, for balance, it's good to choose a spread of goals that cover different areas of your life, such as health, wealth, adventure, work or home. Place one goal in each of the boxes marked *Sub Goals* positioned on either side of your *Main Goal*. As before write them in *Positive*, *Personal*, and *Present* tense with a maximum of ten words on each as in the example Goal Map.

You can have as many goals as you desire. It's only for the purpose of teaching the Goal Mapping technique that I want it kept to five. In later chapters I'll show you how to add others to your existing Map, or create specific Goal Maps focused on just one area of life.

> Once you have a clear picture of your priorities – that is values, goals, and high leverage activities – organize around them.
> **STEPHEN COVEY**

> We will either find a way or make one.
> **HANNIBAL**

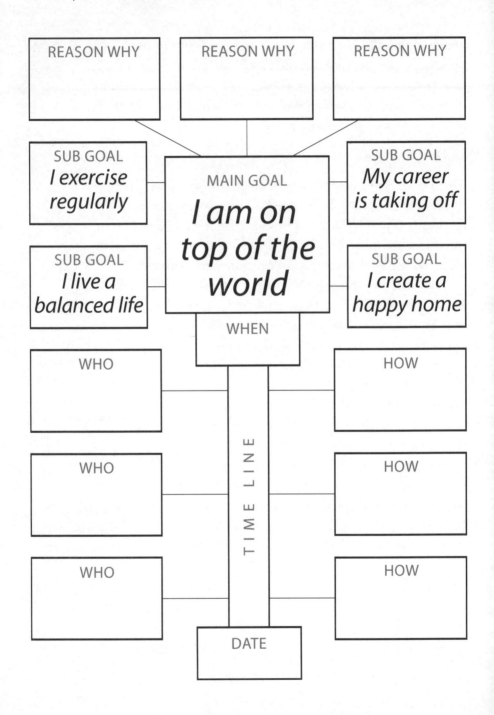

Step 2: Order

Step 3. Draw

What does it look like?

Once you have completed Step 2 by placing your goals in the boxes, it's time to engage in Step 3 and *Draw*. This is the stage that will turn your left-brain written statements into right-brain visual imagery.

Some people on my workshops feel awkward at this point because they have a self-limiting belief about their ability to draw. The truth is that all of us can draw, it's just that some people are more practised and better at it than others. However, your Goal Map doesn't necessarily have to be fine art. You can achieve just as much power using simple stick men or even fundamental symbols such as: ♥✿▲❄✳✤♣◆◇★✶✹♣✱✽✳✶★✿❦❣✿✿✳

A *symbol* conveys more meaning than the image alone represents. For instance, a cross is made up of just two straight lines but can be pregnant with meaning depending whether it is indicating a church, symbolizing a cross-roads or is in the shape of a swastika. Here's the really great news: nobody else needs to be able to understand what your drawing means. You are the only person who needs to know what goals your imagery represents.

Drawing is the language of the right-brain and your right-brain has the main connection to your subconscious. Remember, the effectiveness of any type of intention-setting is to get your goals registered with your subconscious. It's for this reason that the drawing aspect is vitally important.

Goal Mapping requires you to do the drawing yourself, whatever it looks like, because the content of your Goal Map becomes your main command or message. Please don't use clip-art or cut out pictures from a magazine. They may look artistically pleasing but they will not create the same amount of personal power because they haven't been drawn by you and therefore have not activated your brain in the same way.

> A picture is worth a thousand words.
> **AUTHOR UNKNOWN**
>
> If you don't dream you might as well be dead.
> **GEORGE FOREMAN**

Start *now* by drawing a picture or symbol of your Main Goal in the centre space on your right-brain Goal Mapping template (see page 171). You can use a completely blank sheet of paper or card if you prefer, but make sure you leave room for the other steps still to come

Next draw in your Sub Goals on the branches either side of your Main Goal, as in the example Goal Map on page 122. You may want to begin your drawing in pencil, but please use as much colour as possible in the completed version because colour is an excellent right-brain stimulant and carries a strong vibration.

> Some see things as they are and ask why. I dream of things that never were and ask why not?
> **GEORGE BERNARD SHAW**

'Throughout history, the really fundamental changes in societies have come about not from dictates of governments and the results of battles but through vast numbers of people changing their minds – sometimes only a little bit… By deliberately changing the internal image of reality, people can change the world. Perhaps the only limits to the human mind are those we believe in.'

Willis Harman, *Global Mind Change*

Step 3: Draw

Step 4. Why

Why do you want it?

There can be no transforming of darkness into light and of apathy into movement without emotion.

CARL JUNG

Isn't it better to desire to change and live the desire to something higher – than not to desire?

KAHLIL GIBRAN

The heart has its reasons, which reason knows not of.

PASCAL

When your desires are strong enough you will appear to possess superhuman powers to achieve.

NAPOLEON HILL

Goals are simply thoughts that are captured and held on to. What makes a thought powerful is the emotion attached to it, hence Step 4 *Why* is centred on identifying your most powerful emotional reasons for achieving your goals.

Needs are logical (left-brain), but desires are emotional (right-brain). What are the three main emotional reasons for *why* you want to achieve your goals?

Maybe, as in the example Goal Map below, you want a greater level of freedom: to do what you want, when you want, as much as you want. Love is one of the most powerful of emotional motivators and perhaps you desire your goals because of the difference they will bring to somebody else's life as well as your own, such as your partner or family.

Whatever your reasons, they will be unique and special to you. Once you know what they are, state them in the three top boxes of your left-brain template, and then draw them on the three top lines of your right-brain template using pictures or symbols and lots of colour as before.

If you find yourself blocked at this point take a few moments *now* to reconnect with your vision of you living your ideal day, having already achieved your goals. Notice how it feels.

It may take a little while to become clear as to your strongest emotional motivating reasons, but it's worth making the time to reach deep, as you can achieve almost any *What* when you have a strong enough *Why*.

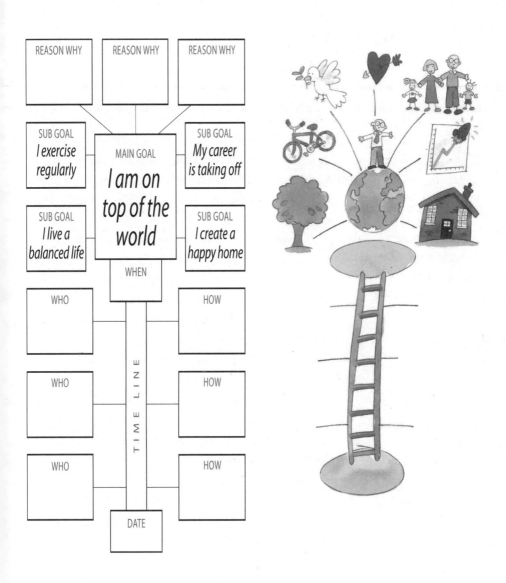

Step 4: Why?

Step 5. When

When do you want it?

So far, the steps you have taken have caused you to work with both your left- and your right-brain. You started with *Dream* and the activation of your right-brain, then *Order* which caused you to work with your left-brain, then back again to your right-brain for *Draw* and *Why*. In Step 5 *When*, you will need to work with both sides of your brain to choose an achievement date for your Main Goal.

Because there are so many uncertainties in life you can go only so far when using your left-brain to try to work out an achievement date, as none of us can be absolutely sure what lies ahead. After you've evaluated a date that makes logical sense, access your right-brain to check if it feels right.

Concentrate on a date for your Main Goal as its very achievement will help the other goals into place. Once you have a date that you are happy with write it in the small circle just below your Main Goal. Now write today's date in the small circle at the bottom of the page.

The parallel lines between the two circles now act as the trunk of your Goal Map on which you can hang Steps 6 and 7. The trunk also serves as a Timeline between your Start date and Achievement date. Many people find it beneficial to divide this timeline into equal sections representing the days, weeks, months or years leading to their goal. Make sure you write the dates on both your left- and right-brain templates.

> Time is our most valuable asset, yet we tend to waste it, kill it, and spend it rather than invest it.
> **JIM ROHN**

> There is a tide in the affairs of men which, taken at the flood, leads on to fortune; omitted, all the voyage of their life is bound in shallows and in miseries.
> **WILLIAM SHAKESPEARE**

> If not you, then who? If not now, then when?
> **HILLEL**

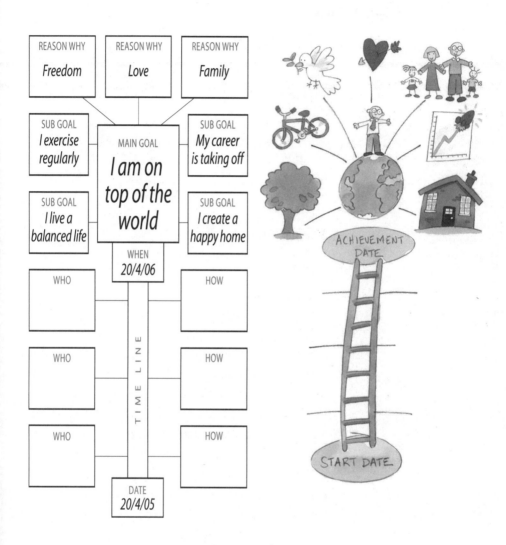

Step 5: When?

Step 6. How

How will you achieve it?

Step 6 *How*, requires you to work with your left-brain again to begin to identify some of the *actions* you will need to take in order to achieve your goals.

Are there new skills you will need to learn?

Will you need to:

◆ search information?

◆ schedule time out?

◆ book a course?

◆ gather resources?

◆ save money?

Life is a unique combination of 'want to' and 'how to', and we need to give equal attention to both.
JIM ROHN

A journey of a thousand miles must begin with a single step.
LAO TSU

Always place the action you can start first on the bottom branch, and then add the others, moving up towards your goals. Once again write statements in the boxes marked *How* on your left-brain template and representational pictures or symbols on the corresponding branches of your right-brain template.

The Goal Mapping templates are designed to capture only your three main actions or *Hows* but in the next chapter it will be explained how you can add more and more detail.

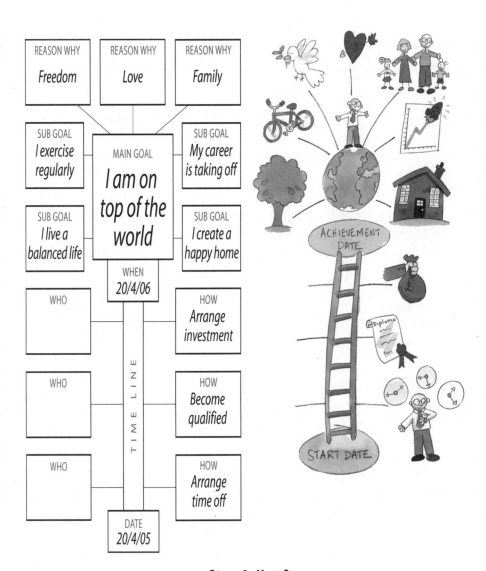

REASON WHY *Freedom*	REASON WHY *Love*	REASON WHY *Family*
SUB GOAL *I exercise regularly*	MAIN GOAL **I am on top of the world**	SUB GOAL *My career is taking off*
SUB GOAL *I live a balanced life*		SUB GOAL *I create a happy home*

WHEN
20/4/06

WHO	TIME LINE	HOW *Arrange investment*
WHO		HOW *Become qualified*
WHO		HOW *Arrange time off*

DATE
20/4/05

Step 6: How?

Step 7. Who

Whose help will you require?

The final step of the Goal Mapping process is Step 7, *Who*. Whose help will you need to achieve your goals? Most large goals will require some sort of advice or assistance. Maybe you will benefit from a role model to help achieve your goal; somebody who has already achieved something similar. If you don't know anyone personally you can always ask others for a recommendation or search for information on the Internet. Maybe a coach or trainer would be useful in helping you; sometimes it can be a friend or relative that serves by giving support and encouragement. Never be afraid to ask for help or advice.

> You cannot hold a torch to light another's path without brightening your own.
> **AUTHOR UNKNOWN**
>
> It takes a lot of courage to show your dreams to someone else.
> **ERMA BOMBECK**

Throughout history the most successful men and women have recognized both their strengths and their limitations and have sought counsel and regular guidance from people they considered more intelligent, better informed, or more enlightened than themselves.

You may decide to put your own name on the branch. If this is the case bear in mind the principle of *Be, Do, Have* that we covered earlier and consider which particular qualities of character or ways of *being* would most serve you in the attainment of your goals.

Once you have identified some of the people whose help you would like, or your own necessary character traits, write them in the boxes marked *Who* on your left-brain Goal Map. Then draw corresponding pictures or symbols on the branches of your right-brain Map. Place the names of people or qualities that you need on branches directly opposite the skill or action that they can help with.

If you want a particular piece of advice or information but don't know who to ask, draw a picture, symbol or key word that represents that advice, and trust that when the time is right your subconscious will attract the information to you.

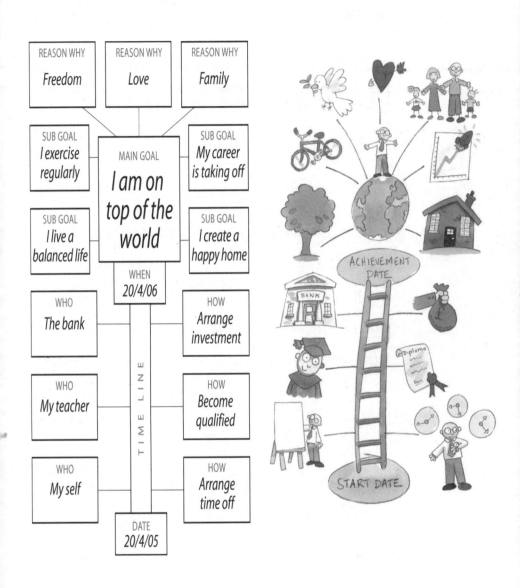

| REASON WHY | REASON WHY | REASON WHY |
| Freedom | Love | Family |

| SUB GOAL | MAIN GOAL | SUB GOAL |
| I exercise regularly | **I am on top of the world** | My career is taking off |

| SUB GOAL | | SUB GOAL |
| I live a balanced life | | I create a happy home |

| | WHEN 20/4/06 | |

| WHO | | HOW |
| The bank | | Arrange investment |

| WHO | TIME LINE | HOW |
| My teacher | | Become qualified |

| WHO | | HOW |
| My self | | Arrange time off |

| | DATE 20/4/05 | |

Step 7: Who?

Chapter 7

The Goal Mapping Ritual

In between where you are, and where you choose to be, is the intermediate state of reaching for your goals. This is achieved through the use of regular effective techniques, or, living by ritual: Sign it – See it – Say it – Feel it – Believe and Achieve it.

Completion and Continuation

A new beginning, with the end in mind.

Congratulations. You have almost reached the end of creating your first Goal Map, which represents the beginning of the new life you have chosen. In the process of producing your Map you have birthed a new attractive thought-form for your future. This you achieved through mental concentration, by envisaging right-brain imagery that represented your left-brain statements, combined with the physical effort of putting pen to paper and drawing your Goal Map. Together these activities helped you to hold your focus and create a new dominant thought command for your subconscious and super-conscious mind. This new *dominant thought* is like a capsule that holds your vision for your future or a seed of tomorrow that you have planted today. It's important to ensure that you continue to nurture the seed, so that your subconscious works with you to grow it, and your super-conscious increasingly attracts it.

This chapter focuses on the Goal Mapping ritual: a number of additional steps you can engage in that will help you boost the power of your Goal Map and increase the manifestation of your desires.

Remember, the higher you raise the energy of your new thought-command above the level of any old, limiting beliefs and self-doubt, the faster your subconscious will work to make your goals come true.

> When you get right down to the root of the meaning of the word 'succeed', you find that it simply means to follow through.
> **F. W. NICHOL**

> Whatsoever a man soweth, that shall he also reap.
> **GALATIANS 6.7**

Sign it

Make a commitment to yourself.

To complete your Goal Map and empower yourself further, all that remains is to *sign it*. Your signature is the mark of your commitment. It is the accepted way of saying that you will keep your word. That's why so many important documents ask for a signature.

Your Goal Map could be one of the most important documents that you'll ever sign, so sign it with real enthusiasm. As you do, make a promise to yourself to keep your word, and follow through with the necessary actions to pursue and achieve your goals.

> To win…you've got to stay in the game.
> **CLAUDE M. BRISTOL**

> Determination is the wake-up call to the human will.
> **ANTHONY ROBBINS**

Commitment

Staying true to yourself.

There are many definitions of commitment and one of my favourites comes from a speaker named George Zaluki, who said: 'True commitment is doing the thing you said you would do, long after the mood in which you said it has left you.'

So many people give their word and make a commitment, and in the moment they actually mean it; but afterwards, for whatever reason, they don't really feel the same way. Their commitment stops being a priority, and often their word is broken altogether.

Keeping your word to your self as well as others is an essential aspect of building your self-esteem and generating greater levels of self-belief and confidence. It is your real power in life. It builds trust, generates respect, and creates synergy.

There is nothing more powerful than someone who follows their words through with actions and does what they say they will. In contrast, there is nothing more disappointing than someone who says a great deal, but rarely follows though with any consistent action, and actually does very little.

Failed in business at age 31.
Was defeated in a legislative race at 32.
Failed again in business at age 34.
Overcame the death of his sweetheart at 35.
Had a nervous breakdown at 36.
Lost an electional race at age 38.
Lost a congressional race at age 43.
Lost a congressional race at age 46.
Lost a congressional race at age 48.
Lost a senatorial race at age 55.
Failed in an effort to become vice-president at age 56.
Lost a senatorial race at age 58.
At the age of 60, Abraham Lincoln was elected President of the United States.

THE PROGRESS OF ABRAHAM LINCOLN

Lasting Commitment

The glue of achievement.

While I've always known at some level that being able to make and stick to a commitment is really important, the reality is that in years past I've found it really quite difficult to make and keep strong commitments.

This has been particularly true when trying to

overcome deeply ingrained habits that had a strong hold on me, such as smoking. I told myself on numerous occasions that the cigarette I was smoking was going to be my last, only to find myself smoking another a few days later. The more often I broke my word to myself, the worse it became, to the point where I became so weak that I would promise myself in the morning, and then break my word to myself by smoking in the afternoon. Sometimes I found it hard to make any kind of commitment at all.

However, the more you persevere with something and the more often you question yourself, the more you learn and the deeper your determination becomes. Gradually, you will find a way forward. Some of the main things that have helped me build my commitment 'muscle' are:

◆ Having a reason – a deeper belief – that goes beyond me.

◆ Understanding that setbacks and failures are learning experiences and part of success.

◆ Remaining conscious of my reasons for making a commitment in the first place.

◆ Finding the courage to make my commitment public. It's usually much harder to break your word to others than to yourself.

◆ Realizing that commitment is not a one-off promise, but rather an ongoing moment-to-moment choice.

> He who has a why to live for can bear almost any how.
> **FRIEDRICH NIETZSCHE**

> It is in your moments of decision that you destiny is shaped.
> **ANTHONY ROBBINS**

Make the Choice

The last point, that commitment is an ongoing choice, was a major factor for me because I was deeply engaged in believing the reverse. I saw commitment as a one-off, isolated act.

In reality, the way that you make a commitment and keep your word to yourself, or anyone else for that matter, is by repeatedly choosing to do so: each day, each moment, each time you are presented with an opportunity to break your word and choose something different. True commitment is an ongoing process, not a casual promise.

I discovered that one of the great benefits of this new way of looking at commitment was that if I did break my word and did something that I said I wouldn't, I found I could quickly re-commit myself again and get back on track. I would look positively at how long I had managed to stick to my commitment, and whatever length of time it was, I would tell myself that I could manage even longer the next time if I re-committed. In this way my commitment grew stronger each time, until I was able eventually to overcome whatever challenge I was facing and stick to my intentions without constant conscious effort.

In contrast to the above, my old and unsuccessful approach to commitment was the complete opposite. I treated commitment as a one-off act that, once lost, was ended. This meant that when I slipped up my attitude worsened and became: 'Oh well, what's the point of trying further. I've done it now, might as well have another, or even the whole packet.' Before I knew it, I'd spiral downwards in energy and go straight back into the same old habit pattern.

If you, like me, have struggled with making commitments or sticking to your word, review the five key points above, and perhaps experiment by making those commitments you find difficult into more of a game.

As long as it's not detrimental to your health or anyone else, and is genuinely for your own highest good, lighten up a little and practise making a promise to yourself to stay committed for just an hour, a day, a week, or month, whatever feels right, and see if that works better for you. You will gradually build up your positive thought habit in this way.

> The greatest power ever bestowed upon mankind is the power of choice.
> Choose to persist without exception.
> Hold fast to your dreams and stay the course, even in the face of exhaustion, rejection, and uncertainty.
> **ANDY ANDREWS**

> We must first make our habits, and then our habits make us.
> **JOHN DRYDEN**

Some people suggest that this is a 'cop out'. A man on my workshop once protested that if he was to follow this approach he would be too soft and just let himself off the hook every time, thereby continuing with something that he knew he should change.

I've heard this many times from all manner of people, and it's also something that I recognize from my past. However, I've learned that you don't make progress by beating yourself up; that just lowers your self-esteem and with it your characteristics of commitment and persistence. In addition it is vitally important to stay mindful of the fundamental principle at play here: that which we resist – persists.

If you are heavily or emotionally committed to something that you are trying to *resist* (for example: cigarettes) then the act of resistance will reinforce your focus and your attachment – which means that you will create or attract more of what you want to resist. The conflicting energies of resistance and attraction become a draining downward spiral, where thoughts of failure result in ever-lower levels of self-esteem and, in turn, reduced ability to stay committed.

> Accept everything about yourself – I mean everything. You are you and that is the beginning and the end – no apologies, no regrets.
> **CLARK MOUSTAKAS**
>
> Much rain wears the marble.
> **WILLIAM SHAKESPEARE**

An Upward Spiral

Your word to yourself is the strongest bond of all.

In contrast to the above, each time you succeed in keeping your word to yourself, even if that is only for an hour, you will exercise what I call your commitment muscle and direct your self-esteem in an upward cycle.

Understand, this is not about making a commitment for a day, and only lasting an hour. This approach works when you make your commitment for an hour, and you stay committed and keep your word for an hour.

Each time you succeed in doing this, you exercise your commitment muscle and grow stronger. Then, choose to make another commitment and stretch yourself a little by going slightly further. For instance, if you are comfortable with an hour, go for two hours, when comfortable with two, go for three, or a whole day, week, and onto a month. In this way you gradually strengthen your commitment, build your self-esteem, and with it create an unbreakable iron will.

See it

Visualize your Goal Map.

> A winner never quits and a quitter never wins.
>
> **AUTHOR UNKNOWN**
>
> Where there is no vision, the people perish.
>
> **PROVERBS 29.18**

Being able to make a commitment and stick to it is vital for achieving your goals, because their achievement will invariably mean paying some sort of price, either in time, effort, or resources. The bigger your goals the greater the price to be paid. However, as another great speaker, Jim Rohn, puts it so succinctly: 'People are prepared to pay the price if the promise is clear. But if the promise isn't clear, the price is always too high.'

When you remain conscious of your vision for your future, and in particular of the reasons *why* you want it, you'll hold true to your promise to yourself and pay whatever price is needed to pursue your goals. If you lose sight of your dream through the fog of self-doubt, any price of effort will always seem too high, your commitment will wane, and your word will be broken.

Help yourself to stay conscious of what is most important to you by viewing your Goal Map everyday. Looking and really seeing is part of the physical act of re-committing yourself. It is a demonstration of your belief in your self and your goals.

Place your Goal Map somewhere that you'll see it regularly. As I am away from home a great deal I carry my main Goal Map with me in my notebook. However over the years my favourite Map spots have been on my bedroom wall or fridge door. These are important spots because I am able to look at it just before I go to sleep at night and again when I first wake in the morning. These are the prime times for reviewing your goals because at these times your brain is in the most receptive state, called alpha rhythm.

Alpha rhythm

Your brain operates on several different frequency vibrations or rhythms at different points through the day. First thing in the morning and last thing at night your brain is in 'alpha rhythm' and it's estimated that in this mental state the connection with your subconscious is up to 100 times greater than it is at midday. Alpha rhythm is the state of mind that you enter while meditating or are under hypnosis. It is the mental state where you heal yourself the most, learn the most, and have your best ideas or intuition. You enter this state naturally first thing in the morning and last thing at night.

Just a few moments invested in looking at your Goal Map while you're in alpha rhythm has the effect of overriding any self-doubt and reinforcing your goal command to your subconscious, as well as reminding you consciously of what you have chosen. This is a really important part of the Goal Mapping ritual and brings great rewards to those who make it a habit.

In my training work with large organizations I run a four-part workshop called 'The Personal Leadership Programme'. The main theme of the programme is that: true leadership is not really about what you *do*, it's much more about who you are choosing to *be*, such as *motivated* and *committed*. That is what makes the biggest difference to what you do and thereby the results you *have*.

> People of mediocre ability sometimes achieve outstanding success because they don't know when to quit. Most people succeed because they are determined to.
> **GEORGE E. ALLEN**

> It is not how much you do, but how much Love you put into the doing that matters.
> **MOTHER TERESA**

The four days of the workshop are usually scheduled at three-month intervals, with Goal Mapping being the foundational module. At the end of the first workshop everyone leaves with a completed Goal Map, and one of the last recommendations I make is that each person should place their Map somewhere that they will see and *view it* for a few moments each day until our next workshop.

When we get together again three months later I can always tell who in the group has followed through and viewed their Goal Map regularly, because they are the people with the beaming faces, with their Map out in front of them. They are the people who can't wait to tell me about all they've achieved since we were last together.

In contrast, the story I hear from the majority of the others is usually that they felt motivated and inspired when leaving the last workshop, but that due to some sort of pressure or crisis in their life they lost touch with the material, their positive feelings and their good intentions, and slipped back into old and often negative habit patterns.

When I ask them if they have viewed their Goal Maps as requested, I find they very rarely have. Often they don't even know where their Maps are. The stories range from: 'I've been too busy', 'I think it might be in the back of a drawer', or 'I've lost it', to my all-time favourite: 'The dog ate it'.

These were the same people who left the first workshop feeling their goals were really important; but they didn't continue to reinforce them, so their focus became distracted by something else.

The Goal Mapping technique works, and works really well, but *you* must work it. Your Goal Map is simply a way of focusing and increasing your natural creative energy, but it does require your input, otherwise there is little to increase. Looking at your

> Winners are those people who make a habit of doing the things losers are uncomfortable doing.
>
> **ED FOREMAN**

> Sow an act, and you reap a habit. Sow a habit, and you reap a character. Sow a character, and you reap a destiny.
>
> **CHARLES READE**

Goal Map once a day boosts your power immeasurably and turbo-charges your ability to manifest to a higher level all together.

Holding the Vision

What I am recommending here as a way of attaining your heartfelt desires is not some new fad or passing fancy. For thousands of years, cultures around the world and virtually all religions have used different types of imagery, symbols and trance states in ritual to influence creation and practise conscious manifestation.

The *Tantric* teachings of India, which have influenced many other cultures and religions, use imagery and symbolism as a core part of their approach. The teachings, which are centred on self-evolution and conscious creation, rely heavily on symbolic drawings and carvings called *Yantra*, which are visual power patterns used as a way of both *holding* and *expanding* consciousness.

A central aspect of the ancient Tantric teaching, and of modern quantum physics, is that all of creation is made from energy held in varying states of vibration. From a central point of perfect cosmic balance energy radiates out in vibrational layers forming atoms, which in turn form everything else that we see, feel, taste, hear and smell. Everything is connected to, and has its reflection in, everything else. For instance every form is just a point on the vibrationary scale, and therefore has its own corresponding *sound* and *colour*.

The principle that everything is connected to everything else, is central to virtually all of the ancient mystery teachings, and led to the practise of using symbols for manifestation.

> The first step to becoming is to will it.
> **MOTHER TERESA**
>
> I tell you this: all you see in your world is the outcome of your idea about it.
> **NEALE DONALD WALSCH**

By creating a visual image or representation of your intention you are in essence holding that energy. It is like creating a mould for the energy of the goal to grow into, just as, if you could see an acorn at an energy level, you would observe a stream of dancing particles being attracted into the acorn and moulded into a mighty oak tree. Applying the same principles, the more often you look at your Goal Map and visualize your intention *as already achieved* the greater the energy you build and the stronger your intention grows, bringing your goal forth into manifestation.

Say it

Affirm your Goal Map.

Just as Yantra is a power image within the Tantric teachings, so a *Mantra* is the sound equivalent. All thought is energy and carries vibration, but a thought that is verbalized into audible sound rises to a much more powerful energy level.

If drawing your Goal Map holds your thought and creates the initial power, viewing or *visualizing* your Map increases the power further. The next step is to say or *affirm* your goal, which raises the vibration and energy even higher.

By repeatedly *affirming* your goal in the form of a Mantra, i.e. stating your goals out loud in *personal*, *positive* and *present* tense, you build the positive energy. If you do this at the same time as visualizing your Goal Map, which is like having your own personal power pattern or Yantra, the effect is even stronger. At a conscious level this practise helps you clarify your goals, while at a subconscious level it reinforces your dominant subconscious command. At a super-conscious level it invokes the universal law of attraction.

Feel it

Feeling the future

Once completed, your Goal Map will take on your energy. Commit yourself to boosting your subconscious power by focusing your attention on your Goal Map once a day, while at the same time affirming your goal out loud. Energy flows where attention goes, and used in this way your Goal Map becomes a funnel and filter for your creative energies as they reach out into the universe.

Chapter 2 looks at the ways in which emotion adds energy to our actions, by empowering both thought and language. Whether expressed via pictures or words, your emotions energize your thought commands and increase the likelihood of you realizing your dreams. To raise the vibrational energy of your Map and your ability to achieve your goals still further, make sure that after you *see it* and *say it*, you really *feel it*.

> Find yourself a quiet space first thing in the morning, even if that space is only inside your head.
>
> ◆ *See it* – Make a moment to imagine yourself achieving your goals.
>
> ◆ *Say it* – As you voice your goals out loud, *feel* what it would be like to actually live as if your goals have been achieved.
>
> ◆ *Feel it* – Project your emotions into the present moment. Allow yourself to really *feel* the emotions and sensations and, as you do so, you will anchor your future intentions into the *now*.
>
> This is the same basic process as re-living a strong memory from your past, only the process is in reverse. Live your chosen future in the now by seeing it, saying it and feeling it.

> To learn anything fast and effectively you have to see it, hear it and feel it.
> **TONY STOCKWELL**
>
> He who reigns within himself and rules his passions, desires, and fears is more than a king.
> **JOHN MILTON**

Finally, unite the three steps into one with your breath:

◆ Begin by looking at your Goal Map and breathe in as you did when initially visualizing you goals: twice in through the nose, all the way down to your stomach; then picture your Goal Map, and affirm your goal as you breathe out slowly through your mouth.

◆ Repeat this process for each goal, reason, and action on your Map. Breathe in through your nose while viewing each point on your Map, then visualize and affirm while exhaling out through your mouth.

It might seem a little strange at first, but this exercise is a great way to take your mind deeper into alpha rhythm, and that means creating a stronger connection with your subconscious; it also helps you to hold your focus and gain conscious clarity. The 10,000,000,000,000,000, 000,000 atoms contained in each lungful of breath then become harmonized with your intentions and encoded with your personal energy, before being exhaled out into the universe – thus creating attraction.

> Practice and thought might gradually forge many an art.
> VIRGIL

This ritual takes only a few moments but has a multitude of benefits. It is both calming and relaxing, and really focuses your mind on your goals, bringing you deeper and deeper levels of insight.

Believe and Achieve it

Demonstrating active faith.

Building your belief in yourself is the prime objective of any form of goal achievement. Your level of belief equals your power to create your desires. Total belief in yourself results in complete power of manifestation.

By following the steps mentioned above and engaging in the Goal Mapping ritual: *re-commit*, *visualize*, *affirm* and *feel*, you will begin naturally to build your self-belief. To ensure you maintain it I have one final recommendation to add to the ritual: engage in a demonstration of *active faith* in your self. Active faith is a physical display of your belief in yourself focused into actions. By thought, word, and *deed*, we create our world. Never leave the site of setting a goal without demonstrating your faith in yourself by taking some form of positive action.

It may be that the majority of physical actions needed to achieve your goal will require some time to organize. But there is always something that you can *do*. Start making some phone calls, arrange to meet or talk to some of the people you have chosen to help you, book some courses or order up some information.

> A firm belief attracts facts. They come out of holes in the ground and cracks in the wall to support the belief, but they run away from doubt.
> **FINLEY PETER DUNNE**

> We are what we repeatedly do. Excellence, then, is not an act, but a habit.
> **ARISTOTLE**

The Challenge

One of the best things that I've ever done to reinforce my goals is to prepare myself by embarking on a thirteen-day mental challenge.

The challenge is simple: to think, feel, and act positively for thirteen consecutive days. Only thirteen days in a row will do. If you break even one day, even at number eleven or twelve you must start back at day one again. You are allowed no more than one minute of negativity in any instance. In that time you must realize you are being negative and change your state to positive.

How do you do that? Simply by following the steps that we've already covered by choosing to focus

> Once the principle of movement has been supplied, one thing follows after another without interruption.
> **ARISTOTLE**

on the positive. You've already identified and recorded some of your most positive thoughts and feelings in the form of a Goal Map. Therefore if you want to take the challenge, all you will need to do to change your state from negative to positive will be to visualize your goals.

Creating a Shift

When I was first offered the thirteen-day challenge by one of my mentors, my response was that I was already very positive and didn't need to do it. 'Good,' my mentor said, 'then it will be really easy for you.'

> The task before us is to silence the negative and the 'I can't', and to build the 'I can'.
>
> **JACK BLACK**

I have to tell you that I didn't find it at all easy. I found it really quite hard. The first time I tried it I got to day three before breaking down into negativity and sadness. I started again and got to day seven. In total, it took me several attempts and many days before I managed thirteen days in a row. However the positive effect of this was well worth the effort.

Thirteen consecutive days is enough time to create a new habit pattern, mentally, emotionally, and physically. Once I had made it through the challenge, it created a total shift in my vision, attitude and action, and I never again saw the world or myself in quite the same way.

Chapter 8

Focusing Your Goal Map

The achievement of any goal is a journey; along the way the scenery will invariably change.

Insight

Gaining clarity and distinction.

Life is dynamic, and the path that leads towards your goals will unfold organically. As you *involve* yourself in the Goal Mapping process and ritual, so your awareness will invariably *evolve* to new heights, bringing new insights and actions for the achievement of your objectives.

Sometimes these insights will relate to comparatively minor details, and sometimes they will represent more wide-reaching developments. Some people even come to realize that some of the goals they are pursuing aren't what they really want at all, and decide to change them completely.

Regardless of the nature or depth of insight you may receive, the same basic principles of 'consciously commanding' your subconscious genie

> Change has a bad reputation in our society. But it isn't all bad, not by any means. In fact, change is necessary in life, to keep us moving, to keep us growing, to keep us interested. Imagine life without change. It would be static, boring, dull.
> **DR DENNIS O'GRADY**

apply. You will want therefore to capture any new information or insights and integrate them into your Goal Map.

Extensions

Capturing and expanding.

It is not uncommon for someone to finish creating their first Goal Map, only to decide that they want to start again, to create a new one. This is usually the result of the drawing process in Goal Mapping stimulating the right-brain, which in turn brings fresh ideas and inspiration.

> When an inner situation is not made conscious, it appears outside as fate.
>
> **C.G. Jung**
>
> When I look into the future, it's so bright it burns my eyes.
>
> **Oprah Winfrey**

The very act of creating your Goal Map will often result in all manner of new realizations, such as expressing your goals with more defining imagery, or adding additional *goals*, *reasons*, or *actions*.

If you feel motivated to completely re-draw your Goal Map, then I urge you strongly to follow through with your heart and begin again. This process will serve you in many ways, not least of which will be to ingrain your commands more deeply in your subconscious.

However, if you are pleased with your Map and want merely to add a few new goals, reasons, or actions, then I suggest you extend your existing Goal Map by following the simple process outlined below.

Adding detail to your Goal Map is like bringing your dream into focus. Adding to your Map actually helps keep it alive and growing. It's an easy and quick process achieved simply by attaching another piece of paper to the side, bottom or top, of your existing Goal Map, and then expanding your text and imagery. In this way you can keep on adding to your Map and grow it organically in line with your expanding awareness.

Growing Your Goal Map

Adding extras: reasons, goals or actions.

If you want to add another motivating reason (a *Why*) to your Goal Map, simply attach a new sheet of paper to the top using sticky tape or glue. Then, draw a branch from the circle around your Main Goal onto the new page, and place your pictures or symbols to represent your new *Why*.

To ensure you maintain your left-brain/right-brain balance, go also to your 'left-brain template' to add another box or write at the side of your existing ones, stating your new motivating reason in words.

You can follow this same basic process for adding other goals. Write your goals as affirmations in boxes on your 'left-brain template', adding more paper if required. Then fix extra paper to the side of your Goal Map, extend a branch from either your Main Goal or Sub Goal, and draw in your new picture.

In like manner you can add more detail to any of your actions (*Hows*). Each action identified is actually a mini goal in itself – it is simply smaller than the other goals and achieved sooner.

If you want to add a single insight or a small amount of detail to an existing action, this is best achieved by drawing in a 'sub-branch' from the existing *How* branch.

At other times you may have a *How* action that is sufficiently large that it warrants breaking down into much more detail and approaching as a goal in its own right. This will be especially true for long-term Goal Maps where major actions or tasks lead towards the achievement of a large or complex Main Goal.

In my office I have a five-year Goal Map showing my vision for all the different areas of my work. Because I know that many things will change

> The future is not some place we are going, but one we are creating. The paths are not to be found, but made. And the activity of making them changes both the maker and their destination.
> **JOHN SCHAAR**

> Learn to see things as they really are, not as we imagine they are.
> **VERNON HOWARD**

> The actions of men are the best interpreters of their thoughts.
> **JOHN LOCKE**

> All who have accomplished great things have had a great aim, have fixed their gaze on a goal which was high, one which sometimes seemed impossible.
>
> **ORISON SWETT MARDEN**

between now and five years' time, I've drawn the Map on a large sheet of card, so there is plenty of room to expand and add to it.

I've drawn the Timeline particularly long so it can carry a greater number of branches and actions; because my Map is drawn to a large scale, it allows me to place a standard calendar 'year planner' next to it. In this way, the *How* branches can point to the relevant dates on the planner and I am able to schedule time for that particular action.

Some of the actions leading to the achievement of my five-year vision represent such large steps in their own right that I've needed to break them down into more manageable objectives by creating mini Goal Maps of each major action. This process really brings Goal Mapping alive as a tool for action planning, and is great for helping you gain brain balance.

How to turn Actions into Goals and Goals into Action

It is useful to break down major actions into Goal Maps in their own right so that you are able to hold the detail of your Main Goal in focus. To turn an action (*How*) into a goal (*What*), simply repeat the key steps of the Goal Mapping process again, only this time focus solely on the specific action you've chosen:

◆ Start by writing your chosen action as a Main Goal on a new left-brain template.

◆ Next attach a new sheet of paper to the side of your Goal Map and extend the *How* branch of the action you want to work on, out into the middle of the blank paper.

◆ Draw a circle at the end of the new branch to signify that your action is now a goal. Make the circle big enough to place an image in it if desired.

> Do the next thing.
>
> **JOHN WANAMAKER**

◆ Next add the individual achievement date, start date, and timeline (the trunk), connecting the dates.

◆ Write in the boxes of your left-brain template and add images to represent the new levels of action to the branches on the right side of the timeline.

◆ Fill in the boxes and, where appropriate, add the names of people who are involved at this deeper level of detail to branches on the left of your Goal Map trunk.

Map extension

Fractals of Success

A 'fractal' is a naturally forming pattern that is *self-similar*, and can repeat many times. For instance the shape of a tree is fractal: break off a branch, hold it upright, and it becomes a mini tree itself; break off a smaller branch and you can repeat the process over and over again. Fractals are nature's way of telling itself how to be.

> Making the simple complicated is commonplace; making the complicated simple, awesomely simple, that's creative.
>
> **CHARLES MINGUS**

In like manner your Goal Map is also a fractal, a repeating pattern created by following the principles of success. You can continue to add more and more detail to any aspect of your Goal Map. Some people even choose to add 'roots' at the bottom showing the things that they've already achieved. The more you add, the more you define, and the more you create.

Specific Goal Maps

Projects, home, health and wealth.

So far you have been guided through a process of creating a 'whole life' Goal Map covering core areas of importance in your life. However, you can also create very specific and focused Goal Maps for individual objectives.

Goal Maps are used by all manner of people and organizations in a range of specific applications. I use the technique for finite objectives such as writing books, and ongoing projects like running my business. When my partner Sangeeta and I decided to get married we created a Goal Map for our wedding, which not only helped us to plan the event, but we liked our Map so much, we also used it as a picture on all of our guest invitations.

> Singleness of purpose is one of the chief essentials for success in life, no matter what may be one's aim.
>
> **JOHN D. ROCKEFELLER**

After we were married Goal Mapping helped us find and own the home we now live in. Our Map detailed all the various aspects and qualities that were important to us in the home we wanted, and what actions were needed in order to acquire it.

Creating the Map helped us to identify what we valued most in a home, such as an open fire and a sense of space, and also to balance these factors with important practical considerations, such as good location for ease of travel and room for us to set up our office.

In addition to all the usual conscious and subconscious benefits, the Goal Map itself proved to be a great way of evaluating quickly the various houses that were offered to us, simply by checking the detail against our dream. However, the home we now live in was found totally on impulse, driven by my subconscious.

We had spent yet another day looking at several houses across a wide area and didn't feel that any of them were right, when Sangeeta said with some frustration, 'Find us our home.' I instantly picked up a paper that was open on the floor, and there it was, right in front of me; though you would never have guessed it from the picture in the advert. In the paper it looked quite awful: dark and dingy. But deep down I knew instinctively that it was the one.

On visiting the house a few days later several parts did indeed look pretty awful and it had been a little neglected. However it matched the important aspects of our Goal Map, and through our Map we were able to see the future potential of the property and the great home it could become with just a little work and effort.

> The greatest potential of control tends to exist at the point where action takes place.
> **LOUIS A. ALLEN**
>
> The great end of life is not knowledge, but action.
> **ALDOUS HUXLEY**

Our offer was accepted and we continued to use the Goal Map to help us follow through with the various actions required to set up home, such as arranging the mortgage, instructing the solicitors, and contracting the movers.

Everything went smoothly and a little while after moving in we created another Goal Map, this time of the extensions and improvements we wanted to make. This new 'home improvements' Map has served not only to help us gain conscious clarity about what we want our home to look like, as a subconscious motivator to start the process, but also as an overview; a 'working plan' for all the various actions needed in arranging and coordinating the building work. I found it really useful to use the Goal Map to check what needed to be done first, who would be responsible for doing it, and when it would need to be started and completed by.

If you need to plan a project or want to create a focused Goal Map for something specific, simply follow the seven steps of Goal Mapping as before, only this time focus your attention on just the main objective or project.

> Patience and perseverance have a magical effect before which difficulties disappear and obstacles vanish.
>
> **JOHN QUINCY ADAMS**

Creating a Project-led Goal Map

Step 1: Dream

Relax and imagine your project or objective as if it is already achieved. *Picture* in your mind what it would look like, take a walk around it, see all the important details, and then note them down on paper as key points or goals.

Step 2: Order

Identify one key point or goal that most clearly defines your project, and write it as an affirmation in the Main Goal box of a left-brain template. Any other points or goals can then be written as the Sub Goals and will serve by giving greater detail and distinctiveness to your project.

Step 3: Draw

Following the layout of a right-brain template, create pictures or symbols that represent your Main Goal and Sub Goals as per regular Goal Mapping. (See Chapter 6 for a reminder.)

Step 4: Why

Typically this step involves capturing the reasons for your personal motivation, however, when used for specific projects it can be used to identify the *benefits* of doing the work, and may sometimes relate to an entire group of people.

> Success is never final.
> **WINSTON CHURCHILL**

Steps 5, 6, and 7: When, How, Who

The final steps are the same as in standard Goal Mapping – simply write the detail of your *When, How* and *Who* in your left-brain template, and then draw the images for your right-brain Goal Map.

Personal Applications

Following the sequence of steps in Goal Mapping is so intrinsic to personal success that it can be used in countless different applications. A growing number of specialists have adopted the technique and have shared it with others by integrating it within their particular practice.

> In giving advice, seek to help, not please, your friend.
> **SOLON**

Health Mapping

Reminding yourself to be well.

My great friend and teacher Bruna Ferrari, runs amazing workshops from her home and retreat in the mountains of Bologna, Italy. She was the first person to point out to me that Goal Mapping is a fantastic tool for helping people to achieve physical, mental and emotional well-being.

Many people now use and teach the Goal Mapping technique for various health and exercise requirements. The general approach is to create a Goal Map that focuses on achieving your highest level of vitality and energy. The process maps the various aspects that will help you to achieve the central goal of well-being, such as diet plan, exercise programme, self-awareness, self-acceptance, and general life-style improvements.

Creating a Goal Map for Well-being

Step 1: Dream
Use the *Dream* step of the Goal Mapping process to become clear about what a greater level of well-being would look like for you personally. Visualize who you would be as a person, and in what ways your life would be different.

Step 2: Order
The next step will enable you to identify the most important aspect of your well-being. It will often be the one you feel the strongest about. Write it down as your Main Goal in the form of an affirmation. (See page 120 for guidance on how to do this.) Any other points or aspects you have about what well-being would look like for you can then be written and drawn as your Sub Goal.

> There is no excellence in all this world which can be separated from right living.
>
> **DAVID STARR JORDAN**

> Do you want to be right, or do you want to be happy? Forgive yourself and stop punishing yourself.
>
> **LOUISE L. HAY**

Step 3: Draw
The next step is the same as in a regular Goal Map. Use simple, clear and colourful images or symbols that represent your goals.

Step 4: Why
The Why stage will be particularly important because identifying your motivating reasons will help you become clearer and more connected to your self-worth, your life and the beauty of life, which will boost your healing response and well-being automatically.

Step 5: When
With a goal like attaining well-being the *When* will

be naturally ongoing. However, it is still important to have a Start Date and a Timeline that form the Goal Mapping trunk.

Step 6: How

The *How* branches connect the Goal Map trunk to the various actions. Sometimes these will be ongoing activities like attending a class or group, and at other times they will represent milestones to aim for, such as: achieving a certain clothes' size, attaining your ideal weight, or reaching a higher level of energy or mobility.

> Life does not require us to make good; it asks only that we give our best at each level of experience.
> **HAROLD RUOPP**

Step 7: Who

The final step carries the names of the people you wish to have help from, or very often with this type of focused Map, your own qualities of character that are aligned with achieving well-being.

Goal Mapping Abundance

To use Goal Mapping for creating a greater level of wealth and abundance – in whatever material or spiritual form you aspire to – simply follow the same basic process as above, only this time your main focus will be centred on creating abundance.

Step 1: Dream

Imagine yourself living in total abundance. What would it look like?

Step 2: Order

What's the most important aspect of your vision of abundance? Your level of income, your standard of living, or maybe your attitude towards money? Write it as your Main Goal with any other aspects forming your Sub Goals.

> I've never been poor, only broke. Being poor is a frame of mind. Being broke is only a temporary situation.
> **MIKE TODD**

Step 3: Draw
Create a Goal Map using simple, clear and colourful images.

Step 4: Why
State in both words and pictures your most powerful motivating reasons for attracting abundance.

Step 5: When
Living in abundance, like good health, is an ongoing objective. However there will still be a Start Date, Timeline, and staged-dates for levels of abundance and financial achievement along your journey.

> I'm not afraid of storms, for I'm learning how to sail my ship.
> **LOUISA MAY ALCOTT**

Step 6: How
Identify your chosen strategies for financial freedom such as: debt reduction, savings, and gaining new abilities.

Step 7: Who
Identify the people or qualities of character, beliefs, and attitudes you need to achieve abundance.

Goal Mapping Habits

The process of changing any negative habit and replacing it with an empowering and positive one is fundamentally the same as planning to achieve any other type of goal or objective. The same basic principles apply.

> Ability is what you're capable of doing. Motivation determines what you do. Attitude determines how well you do it.
> **LOU HOLTZ**

Step 1: Dream
Imagine yourself completely free of your habit. How do you feel and what does your behaviour look like?

Step 2: Order
Write an affirmation in your Main Goal box about

being free of your habit; with any new behaviours, habits or life-style changes as your Sub Goals.

Step 3: Draw
Use clear, colourful and compelling imagery.

Step 4: Why
All habits, no matter how self-destructive, have some form of emotional payoff. Make sure your replacement habit gives you equally strong feelings.

Step 5: When
Choose a Start Date, with a Timeline of at least 21 days for your physical actions, thoughts, and feelings to become habitual.

Step 6: How
State your actions for overcoming the habit, such as classes, new routines, or physical substitutions.

Step 7: Who
What will be your most important qualities of character, and whose help will you want; that of family, friends, or possibly a therapist or coach?

> Knowing that you have complete control of your thinking you will recognize the power.
> **MIKHAIL STRABO**

Once complete, engage in the Goal Mapping ritual and visualize your Map at least once a day.

Professional Applications
Building businesses with Goal Mapping.

Goal Mapping has served the business world for many years and in a variety of different ways. Amongst the foremost of these are:

◆ Generating and capturing a vision for an organization, department or team.

◆ Departmental planning, and communication of collective goals.

◆ As an aid to motivation and achieving performance-related targets.

◆ As an ongoing framework for Personal Development Plans.

◆ As a tool for coaching team members.

Goal Mapping is used increasingly by organizations for capturing a vision of a company's future. Often this process shows up missing aspects in the existing business plan. So effective has Goal Mapping proven to be in helping organizations to steer change that many have now adopted the technique as their central goal-setting methodology.

The human resources team gradually integrates the technique into the culture by using it in all collective goals, conference presentations, and for individual employee personal development.

One of the largest communication companies in the world has included Goal Mapping in their induction training. New inductees create a Goal Map of what they intend to achieve with the organization, what they expect back in return, the actions they plan, and whose help they require along the way. A copy of the Map is held by their manager, and then used in their quarterly reviews to evaluate progress.

In this way the Goal Mapping technique can be used as a standard approach for achievement, a universal framework for success, and people generally develop the habit of taking responsibility for their own objectives.

> You can never change things by fighting the existing reality. You must create something which makes the old model obsolete.
>
> **BUCKMINSTER FULLER**

> It's always worthwhile to make others aware of their worth.
>
> **MALCOLM FORBES**

> Don't bother just to be better than your contemporaries or predecessors. Try to be better than yourself.
>
> **WILLIAM FAULKNER**

Educational Applications

Growing little leaders with Goal Mapping.

There can be few finer feelings than knowing you are able to achieve your aims in life and consciously create your own reality. Learning this at an early age is like learning you can create magic; it fills you with wonder for your future and is a life-long gift that will continue to serve over many years, in countless different ways.

I believe that helping children to understand the nature of goals and success is of fundamental importance. A child who doesn't make the link between their behaviour and the impact it has on others – the *causes* and *effects* in their life – grows into a person who is always blaming others for their problems, and doesn't believe in their own power.

Many children don't learn this important lesson and they grow up blaming others for their own failures. As adults they cause pain, not only to themselves and others around them, but to the next generation of children that they bring into the world.

It was my concern for this issue that led me to write the storybook *Sam the Magic Genie* and its sister book *The Seven Magic Keys for Success*. They were intended as ways of teaching the success principles behind Goal Mapping to both children and adults alike. (For more information see the Further Reading section.)

> A child who can set and accomplish a simple goal will become an adult who knows the joy of changing the world.
> **LINDA AND RICHARD EYRE**

> There is no scarcity of opportunity to make a living at what you love to do, there is only scarcity of resolve to make it happen.
> **WAYNE DYER**

Give the Gift

Sharing with others.

As our journey together draws to a close, I would like to ask you to become the teacher of this material. The best way to learn is to share information with someone else: a friend, a family member, or maybe a colleague. I find that it's only when you explain something to someone else in person that you really find out how well you understand it yourself.

Give the gift of Goal Mapping to another person, whether old or young, and help them gain the magic of turning thoughts into things. You don't need to cover all the points (although we do run a train-the-trainer programme for people who want to teach it professionally) simply follow the main approach and use the seven steps of Goal Mapping. This act of kindness is a fine thing to do for another person that, in the process, will deepen your own level of understanding.

The universal law of return and attraction dictates that, like dropping a pebble in a pond, when you do something good for someone else, the ripples travel out and always return, bringing something good for you.

> A true master is not the one with the most students, but the one who creates the most masters. A true leader is not the one with the most followers, but the one who creates the most leaders.
>
> **NEALE DONALD WALSCH**

> Kindness in words creates confidence, kindness in thinking creates profoundness, kindness in feeling creates love.
>
> **LAO TZU**

> I am not bound to win, I am bound to be true. I am not bound to succeed, but I am bound to live up to the light I have.
>
> **ABRAHAM LINCOLN**

A Final Thought

I originally started my journey into personal development as a way to change the *things* in my life that I didn't like. It never dawned on me fully in those early days that this would mean making changes in *myself*. Each step forward into the material life I have chosen has required a step *up* in myself, another effort towards being my best on a more regular basis.

Personal development, or evolution of self to another level of success, is an ongoing process. There is no end destination, merely a sense of direction and a reason to travel.

Many times I have fallen from the path, but I have always found my way back to continue my journey. Goal Mapping and its sister technique Life

Mapping (see Further Reading) have been an invaluable support.

Use your Goal Maps well. Treasure them. They are, after all, a reflection of you and what you deem important in your life. Honour your Map by giving it your attention and action, and you'll honour yourself by keeping your word.

May the upward spiral of opportunity and self-love that this process creates bring you all that you wish for in life, and turn your heartfelt dreams into wonderful lasting realities.

> The path was worn and slippery. My foot slipped from under me, knocking the other out of the way, but I recovered and said to myself, 'It's a slip and not a fall'.
> **ABRAHAM LINCOLN**

Chapter 9

Your Goal Mapping Checklist

Your future is an adventure that lasts a lifetime. Map your best journey.

This summary section has been designed specifically to guide you quickly and easily through the key points to create a new Goal Map.

Life is ever changing. There will be many stages to your journey. Stay green and growing by creating a new Goal Map every six months, even if you haven't fully achieved your previous goals. Even if it means stating the same goals again, create another Map. The benefits of this will be: new insights, clarity, and subconscious reinforcement.

In addition, create specific Goal Maps for projects you are working on for specific areas of your life.

The Seven Principles of LIFT

Solution generator and goal checker.

The seven principles and questions below will help you to find solutions to challenges, clarity about goals, and gain insights into yourself.

> There comes a time in your life when you realize that if you stand still, you will remain at this point forever. You realize that if you fall and stay down, life will pass you by.
> **VICKI SILVERS**

> I'd rather know some of the questions than all of the answers.
> **JAMES THURBER**

Principle 1: Raise Your Awareness

Do you already know what is needed for a solution? Are you clear about where you want to go, what you want to achieve, who you want to be?

Principle 2: Develop Possibility Consciousness

Are you approaching the situation, your life, or yourself, with an open attitude of possibility, or are you judging from the past?

Principle 3: Find Balance

Will pursuing your current path, new opportunity or goal, lead you towards greater or less balance in your life? (Engage in the balance exercise in Chapter 3 if necessary.)

Principle 4: Be on Purpose

What will be the outcome of this solution, life change, or self-development? Will it move you further towards, or away from your purpose?

Principle 5: Become Fully Response-Able

Are you consciously choosing your response to your challenges, your life, and your self? Or are you being reactive?

Principle 6: Maintain a Positive Focus

Is your dominant focus on the solution or the problem; on what you want or what you fear; on your High Self or your Low Self?

Principle 7: Involve to Evolve

Who could help you find a solution or advise you on your path? Do you need to turn within yourself in search of an answer?

> All appears to change when we change.
> **HENRI AMIEL**
>
> Concentration, in its truest, unadulterated form, means being able to focus the mind on one single solitary thing.
> **KOMAR**

7 Steps of Goal Mapping

A simple system for sustainable success.

Please ensure that you engage in all seven steps of the process of creating your Goal Map, even if you think you already know what you want. I also recommend that you download the Goal Mapping templates from www.goalmapping.com, or copy them form the appendix of this book.

Step 1: Dream – What do you want?

Relax, close your eyes, and imagine you have a magical genie at your command that will help you achieve your every wish. Take a walk through your ideal day, and see your life and self exactly as you desire.

Step 2: Order – What's most important?

Note any ideas, insights and goals that you have. Identify the Main Goal: the one that would most help in achieving the others. Write it as an affirmation in the centre box using *personal*, *positive* and *present tense*, and then do the same with the Sub-goals.

> If you want to know the road up the mountain, ask the man who goes back and forth on it.
>
> **ZENRIN**
>
> Nothing can add more power to your life than concentrating all of your energies on a limited set of targets.
>
> **NIDO QUBEIN**

Step 3: Draw – What does it look like?

Place your right-brain template next to your left-brain template, and draw images, pictures and symbols that represent your goals – using as much colour as possible.

Step 4: Why – Why do you want it?

What are the benefits of this achievement? What are your strongest reasons for succeeding? What feelings well up inside you when you envisage yourself living your dream? Capture the feelings in both words and pictures on your templates.

Step 5: When – When do you want it?

How quickly do you want to achieve your projects and goals? Have you allowed enough time logistically? Does the achievement date feel right in your heart?

Step 6: How – How will you achieve it?

What actions will be needed for this project, goal or life change? Will you require new knowledge, new skills or new habits? State them in both words and pictures.

Step 7: Who – Whose help will you require?

Who will have responsibility for the major actions of the project or goal? Who will *you* need to be, in order to make the journey? Record the names and qualities of character in words and pictures.

Living Your Goal Map

Follow the Goal Mapping ritual.

Sign it

Make and re-make a commitment to your self and others.

See it

Visualize your Goal Map every day, first thing in the morning.

Say it

Speak your goals aloud as affirmations when you visualize.

Feel it

Sense how it would feel to achieve your goals and dreams.

Believe it

Repeat this process every day to build belief in yourself.

> Who you are speaks so loudly I can't hear what you're saying.
> RALPH WALDO EMERSON

Appendices

Left-brain Goal Map Template

Right-brain Goal Map Template

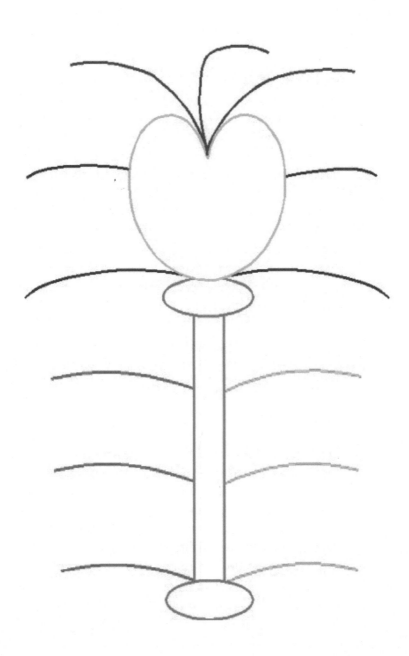

Recommended Reading

Related Titles

Sam The Magic Genie – Brian Mayne (Vermilion, 2003)
The story centres on a young boy who is visited one night by a magical genie called Sam who represents his subconscious. Together they go on an adventure exploring the world of *thoughts* and how they turn into *feelings* and *things*.

The Seven Magic Keys for Success – Brian Mayne. Published by LIFT International ISBN 0-9533161-4-9.
An accompanying book for teachers and parents is called *Seven Magic Keys for Success*. It teaches the seven success principles, together with the Goal Mapping technique, in very simple, child-friendly, 'genie language'.

The *Seven Magic Keys for Success* is ideal for children aged ten years and above, although I have heard from teachers who have taught the basics to children as young as six. It can be taught as a single short overview lesson or as a full course spread over a nine-week period, and is available for both teachers and parents.

Life Mapping – Brian and Sangeeta Mayne (Vermilion, 2002)
Life Mapping is the sister technique to *Goal Mapping* and follows the same basic principles of left-brain words and right-brain pictures, only instead of being focused on the achievement of 'things' *Life Mapping* is dedicated to helping you develop empowering 'qualities of character'.

Together the two techniques cover the fundamental success principle of *Be-Do-Have*:

Be your best in your self, which will naturally lead you to *Do* your best work, and *Have* your best results.

Further Reading

Buzan, Tony, *The Mind Map Book: Radiant Thinking – Major Evolution in Human Thought*, BBC Books, 2000.

Cameron, Julia, *The Artist's Way*, Putnam, 2002.

Coelho, Paulo, *The Alchemist*, HarperCollins, 1991.

Covey, Stephen, *The Seven Habits of Highly Effective People*, Simon & Schuster, 1999.

Dyer, Dr Wayne, *You'll See It When You Believe It: The Way to Your Personal Transformation*, Arrow, 1990.

Frankl, Victor, *Man's Search for Meaning*, Beacon Press, 2000.

Hoff, Benjamin, *The Tao of Pooh*, Methuen, 1984.

Jeffers, Susan, *Feel The Fear And Do It Anyway*, Arrow, 1991.

Johnson, Dr Spencer, *Who Moved My Cheese*, Vermilion, 2002.

McGregor Ross, Hugh, *The Gospel of Thomas*, Watkins, 2002.

Malts, Maxwell, *Psycho Cybernetics*, Simon & Schuster, 1960.

Oakley, Ed and Doug Krug *Enlightened Leadership*, Simon & Schuster, 1994.

Rose, Colin, *Accelerated Learning*, Accelerated Learning Systems Ltd, 1985.

Walsch, Neale Donald, *Conversations with God*, Hodder Mobius, 1997.

Courses and Contact information

Goal Mapping Live (Audio CD)   ISBN 0-9533161-0-6

A 65-minute motivational overview presentation on the power of positive focus and the system of Goal Mapping.

Goal Mapping Pack (Audio CD)   ISBN 0-9533161-1-4

The pack consists of 6 audio CDs and a 50-page workbook with practical exercises, examples and illustrations. Running time approx 4 hrs 30 min

Goal Mapping Workshops, Keynote Presentations, and Trainer Accreditation Programmes are run on a regular basis for businesses, schools, and the general public. If you are interested in attending a presentation or becoming a Goal Mapping practitioner please contact *Lift International*, details below.

To receive our Newsletter (UpLift) or to order any of the above, contact:

Lift International
Goslings, Heathman Street, Nether Wallop, Hants, SO20 8EW England

www.liftinternational.com
info@liftinternational.com
+44 (0)1264 782543

Index